Maiden and Mother

MAIDEN AND MOTHER

Prayers / Hymns / Songs and Devotions

To honour the Blessed Virgin Mary

Throughout the Year

Selected and arranged by

M. M. MILES

IGNATIUS PRESS SAN FRANCISCO

First published in Great Britain in 2001 by
BURNS & OATES
A Continuum imprint
The Tower Building, 11 York Road, London SE1 7NX

First published in the U.S.A. in 2001 by
Ignatius Press, San Francisco

ISBN (UK) 0 86012 305 7
ISBN (USA) 0-89870-780-3
Library of Congress Catalog control number 99-75396

Illustrations by Penelope Harter
Set in 10/12 pt Galliard
a typeface designed by Matthew Carter
Typeset at the Stanbrook Abbey Press, Worcester
Printed in Great Britain by
MPG Books Ltd, Bodmin, Cornwall

CONTENTS

CONTENTS

INTRODUCTION

FEASTS of the Blessed Virgin Mary are major features of both the calendar year and the Church's year, beginning with Advent. The Constitution on the Sacred Liturgy promulgated by the Second Vatican Council reordered the annual cycle of celebrations to enable the faithful to share more deeply in "the whole mystery of Christ as it unfolds throughout the year." In this process, the feasts of the Blessed Virgin Mary were to be emphasized, for she "is joined by an inseparable bond to the saving work of her Son." This tells us that devotion to Mary is not in any way to be downplayed in the post-conciliar Church, and that devotion to the Mother of Jesus is always honour paid to her divine Son.

This collection of prayers, hymns, songs and devotions to honour the Blessed Virgin throughout the year follows the Church's year through its "strong times" of Advent and Christmas, Lent and Easter, and its Ordinary Time throughout the remainder of the year. Both include major celebrations, now known as "solemnities," of the Blessed Virgin, and lesser ones, some observed throughout the universal Church, some locally. The liturgical year begins with Advent, the time of waiting for the saviour to be born to a humble Jewish girl, and during this period she is celebrated in her Immaculate Conception and in the Americas as Our Lady of Guadalupe, defender of the poor and oppressed. Then comes Christmas, with its mystery of Mary as Maiden and Mother, followed now by the great theological Solemnity of Mary, Mother of

God, which begins the calendar year and honours her as *Theotokos*, "God bearer," the unique title used from the fourth century and from which all devotion to her derives. In earlier centuries, the year began on 25 March, the Feast of the Annunciation, the conception of the Lord, nine months before Christmas. Then comes the month of May, Mary's month—for reasons celebrated in poetry here. Summer brings her "birthday into heaven," the Assumption (in the West) or Dormition (in the East), and the year (in the north) declines once more into autumn with her traditional Birthday in September and the month of October devoted to the Rosary.

Prayers and hymns honouring the Blessed Virgin can be traced back as far as the third century, but the Middle Ages, especially the eleventh and twelfth centuries, were the period in which increased reverence for Our Blessed Lady brought many of the most beautiful texts in her honour into being. The first part of the Hail Mary, based on the salutation of the angel Gabriel to Mary and Mary's words to Elizabeth at the Visitation, came into general use in the eleventh century, though its current full form was not generally used before the sixteenth; the *Alma Redemptoris Mater* was composed by Herman Contractus, a Benedictine monk writing in the eleventh century; the *Ave, Regina Caelorum* goes back to St Ephrem in the fourth century; the *Regina Caeli* was composed around the end of the eleventh century (though *The Golden Legend* attributes it, quite unreliably, to St Gregory the Great and angelic voices); the *Salve Regina* is also attributed to Herman Contractus, with its three closing invocations, "O clemens, O pia, O dulcis Virgo Maria," traditionally but probably erroneously attributed to St Bernard, possibly because the prayer was popularized by the Cistercians. It is recorded that Columbus' crew sang it on their voyages to and from America.

During the eleventh century the monasteries flourished, and the Little Office of the Blessed Virgin Mary, modelled on the divine office but considerably shorter, came into widespread use, not only by monks but among pious lay people who could read, especially members of the new Third Orders. It was recommended by St Peter Damian (1007-72), and Pope Urban II ordered it to be said for the success of the First Crusade. Pope Pius V attached an indulgence to its recitation after the Council of Trent, but as Latin became a dead language for the laity, the "Layman's Breviary," as it had been known, fell into relative disuse. In England it was included in the 1850 *Golden Manual, or Guide to Catholic Devotion*, a major early publication of the precursor of the present publisher, Messrs Burns & Lambert. It was re-published in 1914, with a second edition two years later noting its popularity among "young religious," and its vogue lasted up to the liturgical reforms of the early 1960s. It contains a version of the "Hours" of the Breviary, comprising psalms, prayers, hymns, anthems, and blessings for the seven set hours of the day: Matins (with Lauds), Prime, Terce, Sext, None (the four "Little Hours"), Evensong (or Vespers), and Compline. Texts from this, excluding the Psalms, are placed in the Autumn section of this book, to be said during the four weeks of November leading up to Advent. As the 1914 editor wrote, "Through it [the *Gloria Patri* ... said at the end of each psalm] the faithful are constantly reminded that the end and aim of the office is the praise and adoration of the Blessed Trinity. In the Office of our Lady we especially wish to praise and thank the Three Divine Persons for all the great things they have done on behalf of their well-beloved Daughter, Mother, and Bride." The book also recommended a "Way to say the office of the B.V.M.," which can be memorized through its four capital letters:

>Will—hearty;
>Body—reverent;
>Voice—distinct;
>Mind—attentive.

A shorter version also appeared, for the first time in English, in the *Golden Manual*. This was the new "Little Office of the Immaculate Conception," "published by authority at Rome" in 1838, at a time of preparation for the proclamation of the dogma in 1854. In 1977 Irish Messenger Publications of Dublin (subsequently Sacred Heart Messenger) printed a new translation of this in a booklet titled *The Little Office of the Immaculate Conception of The B.V.M.* The Office consists of prayers and hymns to be said or sung in the morning, at mid-morning and noon, in the afternoon and evening, and at night. Its purpose was to encourage Christian families to say the Little Office at home, in line with the wish of the then Pope, Paul VI. Prayers from Dawn to Night taken from this will be found in the Pentecost section, to be said throughout May, Our Lady's Month, and again in Autumn, they may be used throughout October, the month of the Rosary.

By following in the footsteps of such publications, then, this book is intended to encourage a simplified form of liturgical devotion to Mary, and to show how love for her has been expressed throughout the history of the Church and what would be lost if such a rich tradition were to be forgotten. It therefore prints some of the best-loved hymns and prayers in their original Latin as well as in English translations, together with, in some cases, music in either plainchant or modern notation. The Latin words and the music will still be familiar to some, and it is hoped that mainly younger users, to whom they may not be known, will be encouraged to learn them and to play their part—individually or in groups—in keeping a great tradition alive.

ADVENT

The Church's Calendar begins with Advent.
Its liturgical colour is purple,
denoting sorrow for sin and doing penance.
Advent begins on or about 30 November
and always includes four Sundays.

Advent has two feasts of Our Lady:
8 December
The Immaculate Conception of the Blessed Virgin Mary
12 December
Our Lady of Guadalupe

OUR LADY OF GUADALUPE

(see pages 19–23)

ADVENT

To be said every day in Advent, and throughout the year:

Prayer: Hail Mary

Hail Mary, full of grace, the Lord is with thee; blessed art thou among women, and blessed is the fruit of thy womb, Jesus. Holy Mary, Mother of God, pray for us sinners, now, and at the hour of our death. Amen.

In the morning:

O Lady, make speed to befriend me, from the hands of the enemy mightily defend me. Glory be to the Father, and to the Son, and to the Holy Spirit*, as it was in the beginning, is now, and ever shall be, world without end. Amen. Alleluia.

Sweet Lady,
Remember me kindly.

Medieval Benedictine Prayer

* "Spirit" has generally been preferred to the older "Ghost".

3

GAUDE VIRGO MATER CHRISTI

GAUDE virgo mater Christi
Quae te matrem ostendisti
Multis reis corde tristi.
Non est quis quem tu sprevisti
Sua in angustia.

Rejoice, virgin Mother of Christ,
Who offer yourself a mother
To the many sorrowful sinners in your care.
There are none whom you have ever spurned
In their trouble.

Id circo mater miserorum
Respectum feras peccatorum
Non es prona suppressorum
Dare corda compunctorum
Caelis ad miseria.

Therefore, Mother of mercies,
Look upon us sinners,
For you are close to the oppressed
To bring contrite hearts to heaven
Out of their distress.

Nostra spes et advocata,
Cunctis turbis es probata,
Ducens membra venenata
Ad loca per beata
Celsa supra sidera.

Our hope, our advocate,
Proven in the sight of all,

ADVENT

You lead souls poisoned by hell
On to their blessed home
High above the stars.

Quid vereris te curvare
Miser, et hanc exorare,
Tundens pectus, flens amare;
Sciens non vult refutare
Quemquam in tristitia.

Why fear then to kneel,
Wretched we, and pray to her,
Beating our breasts amid bitter tears;
She knows us, and will turn away
No one with true sorrow.

O tu virgo labe carens,
Es labentum semper parens;
Sim et tibi vita parens
Vivens in hoc saeculo.

O Virgin quite without stain,
You are ever a mother to those who fall;
May I in my life be obedient to you
While I live here on earth.

At nos omnes hic degentes
Recurramus huic, dicentes:
Consolate nos gementes
In te nostram spem ponentes
Mortis in periculo.

And let us all who dwell here below
Have recourse to her and say:

5

Comfort us as we cry to you,
For in you we put our hope
As we stand in the fear of death.

Words by William Cornysh (d. 1523)
English translation by Jeremy White (with slight adaptations)

O SANCTISSIMA

O Sanctissima   10.7.01.7   *Sicilian Melody*

O SANCTISSIMA, O piissima,
Dulcis Virgo Maria!
Mater amata, intemerata,
Ora, ora pro nobis.

O most holy one, O most merciful,
O sweet Virgin Mary!
Mother best beloved, Mother undefiled,
Pray, pray for us!

6

Tu solatium et refugium,
Virgo mater Maria!
Quidquid optamus, per te speramus,
Ora, ora pro nobis.

Thou art our comfort and our refuge,
Virgin Mother Mary!
All that we long for, through thee we hope for;
Pray, pray for us!

Ecce debiles, perquam flebiles,
Salva nos, O Maria!
Tolle languores, sana dolores,
Ora, ora pro nobis.

See how weak we are, lost in tears,
Save us, O Mary!
Lighten our anguish, soothe our sorrows,
Pray, pray for us!

Virgo, respice, mater, adspice,
Audi nos, O Maria!
Tu medicinam portas divinam,
Ora, ora pro nobis.

Virgin, turn and look, Mother, behold us;
Hear us, O Mary!
Thou art the bearer of health divine,
Pray, pray for us!

Tua gaudia et suspiria,
Juvent nos, O Maria!
In te speramus, ad te clamamus,
Ora, ora pro nobis.

May thy joys and thy sorrows
Be our help, O Mary!
In thee we hope, to thee we cry,
Pray, pray for us!

ANTHEM: ALMA REDEMPTORIS MATER

From vespers of the Saturday before the first Sunday of Advent
to the feast of the Presentation of the Lord, 2 February:
Solesmes Plainsong

AL-MA * Re-demptóris Ma-ter, quae pérvi-a cae-li

Porta manes, et stella ma-ris, succúrre cadénti

Súrge-re qui cu-rat pópu-lo: Tu quae genu-ísti,

Na-tú-ra mi-ránte, tu-um sanctum Ge-ni-tór-em:

Virgo pri-us ac posté-ri-us, Gabri-é-lis ab o-re

Sumens il-lud Ave, pecca-tó-rum mi-se-ré-re.

Herman Contractus (d. 1054)

8

℣. Angelus Domini nuntiavit Mariae.
℟. Et concepit de Spiritu Sancto.

Oremus:
GRATIAM tuam, quaesumus, Domine, mentibus nostris infunde; ut qui, angelo nuntiante, Christi Filii tui incarnationem cognovimus, per passionem ejus et crucem ad resurrectionis gloriam perducamur. Per eundem Christum Dominum nostrum. Amen.

> *Mother of Christ! Hear thou thy people's cry;*
> *Star of the deep, and Portal of the sky,*
> *Mother of him who thee from nothing made,*
> *Sinking we strive, and call to thee for aid:*
> *Oh, by that joy which Gabriel brought to thee,*
> *Thou Virgin first and last, let us thy mercy see.*

℣. *The angel of the Lord declared unto Mary.*
℟. *And she conceived of the Holy Spirit.*

Let us pray:
Pour forth, we beseech thee, O Lord, thy grace into our hearts;
that we, to whom the incarnation of Christ thy Son was made
known by the message of an angel, may, by his passion and
cross, be brought to the glory of his resurrection. Through the
same Christ our Lord. Amen.

PRAYER

SUB tuum praesidium confugimus, sancta Dei Genitrix; nostras deprecationes ne despicias in necessitatibus nostris; sed a periculis cunctis libera nos, semper Virgo, gloriosa et benedicta.

> *We fly to thy patronage, O holy Mother of God;*
> *do not despise our petitions in our needs;*
> *but deliver us from all dangers,*
> *O ever-virgin, glorious and blessed.*

The earliest known prayer to Our Lady,
not later than the fourth century

꙳

OF THE WORD OF GOD

Del verbo divino
La Virgen preñada
Viene de camino
Si le dais posada.

St John of the Cross, written between 1582 and 1588.

If you meet the Virgin
Coming down the road,
Ask her into your house:
She bears the Word of God.

The Virgin, weighed
with the Word of God,
comes down the road:
if only you'll shelter her.

Translated by Kathleen Jones

10

SALVE REGINA

From first vespers of Trinity Sunday to Advent
Solesmes Plainsong

SALVE Re-gí-na, * ma-ter mi-se-ri-córdi-ae: Vi-ta,

dul-cé-do, et spes nostra, salve.   Ad te clamámus,

exsules fi-li-i Hevae.   Ad te suspi-rámus, geméntes et

flentes in hac lacrimárum valle.   Eia ergo, Advocata

nostra,   il-los tu-os mi-se-ri-córdes ó-cu-los ad nos

convér-te;   et Je-sum, be-ne-díctum fructum ventris

tu-i, no-bis post hoc exsí-li-um   osténde. O cle-mens,

O pi-a, O   dulcis Virgo Ma-rí-a.

Herman Contractus (d. 1054)

11

℣. Ora pro nobis, sancta Dei Genitrix.
℟. Ut digni efficiamur promissionibus Christi.

Oremus:
OMNIPOTENS, sempiterne Deus, qui gloriosae virginis matris Mariae corpus et animam, ut dignum Filii tui habitaculum effici mereretur, Spiritu Sancto cooperante, praeparasti; da, ut cujus commemoratione laetemur, ejus pia intercessione ab instantibus malis et a morte perpetua liberemur. Per eundem Christum Dominum nostrum. Amen.

Hail, holy Queen, Mother of mercy;
hail, our life, our sweetness, and our hope!
To thee do we cry, poor banished children of Eve;
to thee do we send up our sighs,
mourning and weeping in this vale of tears.
Turn then, most gracious Advocate,
thine eyes of mercy towards us
and, after this our exile, show unto us
the blessed fruit of thy womb, Jesus.
O clement, O loving,
O sweet Virgin Mary!

℣. *Pray for us, O holy Mother of God.*
℟. *That we may be made worthy of the promises of Christ.*

Let us pray:
Almighty and everlasting God, who through the power of the
Holy Spirit hast procured in the body and soul of the glorious
Virgin Mother Mary a habitation meet for thy Son's indwelling:
grant that, as we keep her name in joyful remembrance, we

12

may be set free by her loving prayers from the dangers that here beset us, and from everlasting death in the world to come. Through the same Christ our Lord. Amen.

❧

POEM: *De Sancta Maria*

O flos, tu non germinasti de rore
nec de guttis pluviae, nec aer desuper te volavit,
sed divina claritas in nobilissima virga
te produxit.

O virga, floriditatem tuam
Deus in prima die creaturae suae praeviderat.

Et de Verbo suo auram materiam,
O laudabilis virgo, fecit.

To Our Lady

No tender dew, no breeze or shower
But God in all his loving power
Raised you, a branch of his own nation,
To bear the joy of our salvation.
When he first thought of shining bright
With all the radiance of his light,
You were a gleam of his devising
Whose Word in pure gold uprising
We praise with you in every hour,
O fragrant rose and freshest flower.

St Hildegard of Bingen (1098-1179), from Symphonia armonie
celestium revelationum, *trans. John Cumming*

13

Novena Prayer
Recited after vespers during Advent until 8 December:

O MOST pure and immaculate Virgin, the most privileged of all creatures, the only one amongst the descendants of Adam who wert never for an instant an enemy of thy Creator. O most perfect image of the holiness of God, Mary, conceived without sin, remember, we conjure thee, the ends for which thou wert enriched with graces which no mortal before or since has ever enjoyed. Remember thou wert miraculously preserved from even the shadow of sin, not only that thou mightest become the Mother of God, but also the mother, the refuge, and advocate of man; penetrated, therefore, with the most lively confidence in thy never-failing mediation, we most humbly implore thy intercession for obtaining the intentions of this Novena [...]. Thou knowest, O Mary, how often our hearts are the sanctuaries of God, who abhors iniquity. Obtain for us, then, that angelic purity which was thy earliest and favourite virtue, that purity of heart which will attach us to God alone, and that purity of intention which will consecrate every thought, word, and action to his greater glory. Obtain for us also a constant spirit of prayer, silence, and self-denial, that we may recover by penance that innocence which we have lost by sin, and at length attain safely to that blessed abode of saints where nothing defiled can enter.

O Mary, conceived without sin,
Pray for us who have recourse to thee.

From the Little Office of the B.V.M.

8 December
The Immaculate Conception
of the Blessed Virgin Mary

Because God made Mary full of his sanctifying grace and so the greatest of his creatures, she was worthy to be the Mother of Jesus Christ, the Son of God. Unlike us, Mary was born without original sin, but like us she had free will. She chose to listen to God and to be obedient to his will, and she put her whole trust in God. By doing this she acted as God's instrument, the instrument that enabled God to send his only Son down to earth to be the saviour of humankind.

The feast was celebrated in the East by the eighth century and soon after that in the West also. It was known in England and Ireland before the Norman Conquest; in Normandy it was known as the feast of the Normans. It was strongly defended by the Franciscans, especially by Bd Duns Scotus (d. 1308), "who fired France for Mary without spot" (Hopkins). The Franciscan pope Sixtus VI extended it to the universal Church in 1477, and the Immaculate Conception was defined as a dogma in 1854. Formerly a Double of the First Class with Octave, since the Calendar reform of 1969 it ranks as a Solemnity.

I EXULT for joy in the Lord, my soul rejoices in my God; for he has clothed me in the garment of salvation and robed me in the cloak of justice, like a bride adorned with her jewels.

Entrance antiphon at Mass

15

POEM:
The Blessed Virgin compared to the Air we Breathe (excerpt):

> Mary Immaculate,
> Merely a woman, yet
> Whose presence, power is
> Great as no goddess's
> Was deemèd, dreamèd; who
> This one work has to do—
> Let all God's glory through,
> God's glory, which would go
> Through her and from her flow
> Off, and no way but so.

.   .   .

> Of her flesh he took flesh:
> He does take fresh and fresh,
> Though much the mystery how,
> Not flesh but spirit now
> And makes, O marvellous!
> New Nazareths in us,
> Where she shall yet conceive
> Him, morning, noon, and eve;
> New Bethlems, and he born
> There, evening, noon, and morn.

Gerard Manley Hopkins, S.J. (1844-89)

FROM THE MASS

In Conceptione Immaculata Beatae Mariae Virginis
(1854) in the Roman Missal

ALLELUIA

> Alleluia, alleluia. Tota pulchra es, Maria,
> et macula originalis non est in te. Alleluia.

> *Alleluia, alleluia. Thou art all fair, O Mary,*
> *and the stain of original sin is not in thee. Alleluia.*

OFFERTORY ANTIPHON

> Ave Maria, gratia plena: Dominus tecum:
> benedicta tu in mulieribus. Aßlleluia.

> *Hail Mary, full of grace: the Lord is with thee:*
> *blessed art thou among women. Alleluia.*

COMMUNION ANTIPHON

> Gloriosa dicta sunt de te, Maria;
> quia fecit tibi magna qui potens est.

> *Glorious things are told of thee, O Mary,*
> *for he who is mighty hath done great things unto thee.*

❧

The *Salve Regina* (p.11) is sung at the end of Mass.

HYMN

IMMACULATE Mary, our hearts are on fire,
That title so wondrous fills all our desire.
Ave, ave, ave Maria!
Ave, ave, ave Maria!

We pray for God's glory, may his kingdom come,
We pray for his vicar, our father, and Rome.
Ave, ave…

We pray for our mother the Church upon earth,
And bless, sweetest Lady, the land of our birth.
Ave, ave…

For poor, sick, afflicted, thy mercy we crave;
And comfort the dying, thou light of the grave.
Ave, ave…

In grief and temptation, in joy or in pain,
We'll ask thee, our Mother, nor seek thee in vain.
Ave, ave…

In death's solemn moment, our Mother, be nigh;
As children of Mary O teach us to die.
Ave, ave…

And crown thy sweet mercy with this special grace,
To behold soon in heaven God's ravishing face.
Ave, ave…

Now to God be all glory and worship for aye,
And to God's virgin Mother an endless *Ave*.
Ave, ave…

English, nineteenth century, author unknown, sung to
the traditional French melody of the "Lourdes hymn"

12 December
Our Lady of Guadalupe

An apparition of the Virgin is recorded at Guadalupe in Estremadura in south-western Spain in the fourteenth century, when she appeared to a cowherd and asked him, in return for restoring the life of first a cow and then one of his children, to dig on the spot where she had appeared, where a statue of her lay hidden. He told his story to the priests, who found the statue and erected a shrine, as the Virgin had asked.

Two centuries later, an Indian peasant, Juan Diego (now Blessed) was passing a hill named Tepeyac, sacred to the Aztecs, near what is now Mexico City, when he heard his name being called from the hill. He climbed the hill, where he found a "dark girl" (morenita *in Spanish) who said she was the Virgin Mary and that she wanted a shrine built to her on the spot, from which she would help the Indian population of Mexico, oppressed by the Spanish conquerors. After miracles had convinced the bishop, the shrine was built and named after the Virgin of Guadalupe. Under this title Our Lady is venerated as patroness of the Americas, and the shrine, with Juan Diego's* tilma *or Aztec cloak on which the image of Our Lady is imprinted, is visited by many pilgrims throughout the year and is the focus of a massive annual pilgrimage on 12 December.*

(The feast is not celebrated in Europe, but in England, Scotland, and Ireland Our Lady of Guadalupe has been adopted as patroness of unborn children by the Society for the Protection of Unborn Children.)

PRAYERS TO OUR LADY OF GUADALUPE

OUR LADY of Guadalupe, mystical rose, intercede for the Church, protect the Holy Father, help all who invoke you in their necessities.

Since you are the ever-virgin Mary and Mother of the true God, obtain for us from your most holy Son the grace of a firm faith and a sure hope amid the bitterness of life, as well as an ardent love and the precious gift of final perseverance.

MOTHER OF CHRIST, pray for all mothers; may they cherish the gift of their children as you cherished the infant Christ.

Seat of Wisdom, pray for all who govern, that all may learn the true values of life.

Queen of Apostles, pray for our clergy; may they, like your Son, be fearless in proclaiming the truth.

Virgin most powerful, pray for all pro-life workers; may they find strength in moments of darkness.

Comfort of the afflicted, pray for those who care for the sick; may they care for broken people as once you cradled the body of your Son.

Mother of our Saviour, pray for our world; may we love all God's children from the moment of conception.

Queen of all Saints, pray for us all; may our faith be strengthened, that we may continue to work for just laws with hope and trust.

ADVENT

An account of the apparition in Mexico was written in Náhuatl in 1533 by Antonio Valeriano, an Indian pupil of the Jesuits at Tlateloco. It is known as the Nican Mopohua *and relates the following:*

Coming, then, at daybreak to the foot of a little hill known as Tepeyacac ... the Indian heard, on the summit of the hill and on an outcrop of rock raised from the plain on the shore of the lake, a sweet and tuneful song, which, according to him, appeared to be made by a multitude of different sorts of birds, singing together gently and harmoniously, one choir responding to another with excellent timing, their echoes thrown back and repeated by the high summit standing out above the hill; and lifting his eyes to the place from which he thought the singing was coming, he saw on it a white and shining cloud, and around it a beautiful multi-coloured rainbow formed from the rays of an extraordinary light and clarity appearing in the middle of the cloud. The Indian remained absorbed and as though outside himself in a gentle rapture, without the least fear or perturbance, feeling a joy and excitement in his heart that made him ask himself, "What can I be hearing and seeing? Where have I been taken?" [Then] he heard himself being called by his name, Juan, in a woman's voice, sweet and soft, which came from the splendours of that cloud and told him to approach: he went with all speed to the top of the little hill.

In the midst of that light he saw a most beautiful Lady...who spoke to him serenely and in the Mexican language, saying, "My son Juan, whom I love tenderly because you are small and delicate, where are you going?" The Indian replied, "I am going, noble lady and my Lady, to Mexico, to the district of Tlateloco to hear Mass...."

When most holy Mary had heard him, she spoke to him thus: "Know, my son, most beloved, that I am the the ever-virgin Mary, Mother of the true God, Author of life, Creator of all and Lord of heaven and earth, who is everywhere; and it is my wish that a shrine be built for me in this place where, as a merciful mother to you and your people, I will show my loving clemency and the compassion I feel for the natives and for those who love me and seek me, and for all those who implore my help and call on me in their labours and afflictions; and where I shall hear their tears and cries, to give them comfort and relief; and for my wish to come into effect, you must go to the city of Mexico and to the palace of the bishop who resides there, to whom you will say that I send you and that it is my wish that a shrine be built to me in this place...."

Juan went to the bishop, but failed to persuade him. Coming back to the hill, he met the vision again, and, the account says, his words to her deserve to be recorded: "My Girl, most beloved, my Queen and most high lady, I did what you ordered me...I gave him your request in the form you instructed me; he heard me gently and attentively: but, from what I observed in him and from the questions he put to me, I grasped that he had not believed me, because he told me to come back another time, so that he could question me more fully and deeply about this business. He assumed that the shrine you ordered to be built is something I made up or imagined and not your will; and so I ask you to send some noble and important person on this mission, someone worthy-of respect, who should be believed; because, as you can see, my Lady, I am a poor peasant, a humble working man, and this mission is not for me...."

Most holy Mary listened benignly to what the Indian said to her, and having heard him spoke to him thus: "Listen, my well loved son: know that I have no lack of servants to command, who would do what they are told; but it is most fitting that you should carry out this mission and that you should bring about the fulfilment of my will and my wish; and so I ask you, my son, and order you to go back to the bishop tomorrow and tell him to build the shrine I have asked you for and that she who sends you is the Virgin Mary, Mother of the true God."

Trans. from the Spanish by Paul Burns

PRAYER OF ST ALOYSIUS GONZAGA

O MARY, my holy Mistress, into thy blessed trust and special keeping, into thy tender heart this day, every day of my life, and at the hour of my death, I commend my soul and body. To thee I entrust all my trials and miseries, my life and the end of my life, that through thy most holy intercession and thy merits, all my actions may be ordered and disposed according to thy will and that of thy divine Son. Amen.

CHRISTMAS

*The Christmas season in the Church's calendar
lasts from Christmas Day to
the feast of the Baptism of the Lord
(the Sunday after Epiphany).
There are then a few weeks of Ordinary Time
before the beginning of Lent.
The liturgical colour for Christmas is white,
denoting rejoicing.*

*This season and the weeks of Ordinary Time that follow
include these feast days associated with Our Lady:
25 December: The Nativity
First Sunday after Christmas: The Holy Family
1 January: Solemnity of Mary, the Mother of God
2 February: The Presentation of the Lord
11 February: Our Lady of Lourdes*

*If there is no Sunday after Christmas in December,
the feast of the Holy Family
is celebrated on 30 December.*

*During Ordinary Time,
the Saturday Mass of Our Lady can be celebrated
if no solemnity, feast, or obligatory memorial
falls on that particular Saturday.*

THE NATIVITY
*(based on The Prayerbook of Margarete von
Rodemachern – late fifteenth century)*

25 December
The Nativity

MODER OF GOD, wich dyd lappe thy lytel swete babe in clothes, and betwene two beestes in a crybbe layde hym in hey, pray for me that my naked soul maya be lapped in drede and love of my Lorde God and the Alleluya. Ave Maria.

lappe = wrap, clothe   *drede = fear*

LATE MEDIEVAL LYRICS

(i) "The Rose that bare Jesu"

> Ther is no rose of swych vertu
> As is the rose that bare Jesu.
>
> Ther is no rose of swych vertu
> As is the rose that bare Jesu,
> *Alleluya!*
>
> For in this rose conteynyd was
> Heven and erthe in lytyl space,
> *Res miranda!*
>
> By that rose we may weel see
> That he is God in personys thre,
> *Pari forma.*

27

The aungelys sungyn the sheperdes to,
"Gloria in excelsis Deo".
Guadeamus.

Leve we al this wordly merthe,
And folwe we this joyful berthe:
Transeamus.

(ii) The Virgin's Lullaby

'Lullay, lullow, lully, lullay,
Bewy, bewy, lully, lully,
Bewy, lully, lullow, lully,
Lullay, baw, baw, my barne,
Slepe softly now.'

I saw a swete semly shght,
A blisful birde, a blossum bright,
That murnyng made and mirth of-mange;
A maydin moder, mek and myld,
In credil kep a knave child
That softly slepe; scho sat and sange.

murnyng = mourning, lament
of-mange = meanwhile   knave = boy

CHRISTMAS

(iii) Out of Sleep Arise and Wake!
(Verses 1-3, referring to Our Lady)

Nowel, nowel, nowel,
Nowel, nowel, nowel!

Owt of your slepe aryse and wake,
For God mankynd nowe hath ytake
Al of a maide without eny make;
Of al women she bereth the belle.
Nowel!

And thorwe a maide faire and wys
Now men is made of ful grete pris;
Now angelys knelen to mannys servys,
And at this tyme al this byfel.
Nowel!

Now man is brighter than the sonne;
Now man in heven an trye shal wone;
Blessyd be God this game is begonne,
And his moder emperesse of helle.
Nowel!

helle = wellbeing, salvation

H YMNS

I Sing of Mary

SING of Mary, pure and lowly,
Virgin Mother undefiled.
Sing of God's own Son most holy,
Who became her little child.
Fairest child of fairest Mother,
God, the Lord, who came to earth,
Word made flesh, our very brother,
Takes our nature by his birth.

Sing of Jesus, Son of Mary,
In the home at Nazareth.
Toil and labour cannot weary
Love enduring unto death.
Constant was the love he gave her,
Though he went forth from her side,
Forth to preach and heal and suffer,
Till on Calvary he died.

Glory be to God the Father,
Glory be to God the Son;
Glory be to God the Spirit,
Glory to the three in one.
From the heart of blessed Mary,
From all saints the song ascends,
And the Church the strain re-echoes
Unto earth's remotest ends.

Roland Ford Palmer, S.S.J.E., written c. 1914

II As Dew in Aprille

> I SING of a maiden
>   That is makèles:
> King of all Kings
>   To her son she ches.
>
> He came also stille
>   Where his moder was,
> As dew in Aprille
>   That falleth on the grass.
>
> He came also stille
>   To his moder's bour,
> As dew in Aprille
>   That falleth on the flour.
>
> He came also stille
>   There his moder lay,
> As dew in Aprille
>   That falleth on the spray.
>
> Moder and mayden was never none but she:
> Well may such a lady Goddes moder be.
>
> *Anon, 13th century*

III To Our Lady

> COME, gentle Mother of our Redeemer,
>   thou ever-open gate of heaven;
> Come, star of the sea, and help
>   the fallen who seek to rise again.
> Thou who, while nature marvelled,
>   didst give birth to thy own
> All-holy Maker, thyself a virgin first and last,
>   hear once again the angel's greeting,
>   and take pity on all sinners.
>
> *From the Divine Office*

IV Virgin, wholly marvellous

Orientis partibus   77.77   *P. de Corbeil (d. 1222)*

VIRGIN, wholly marvellous,
Who dids't bear God's Son for us,
Worthless is my tongue and weak
Of thy purity to speak.

Who can praise thee as he ought?
Gifts, with every blessing fraught,
Gifts that bring the gifted life,
Thou didst grant us, Maiden-Wife.

32

CHRISTMAS

God became thy lowly Son,
Made himself thy little one,
Raising men to tell thy worth
High in heav'n as here on earth.

Heav'n and earth, and all that is,
Thrill today with ecstasies,
Chanting glory unto thee,
Singing praise with festal glee.

Cherubim with fourfold face
Are no peers of thine in grace;
And the six-wing'd seraphim
Shine, amid thy splendour, dim.

Purer art thou than are all
Heav'nly hosts angelical,
Who delight with pomp and state
On thy beauteous Child to wait.

St Ephrem the Syrian (c. 307-78)
Trans. J. W. Atkinson, S.J. (1866-1921)

The Holy Family

Today's feast gives a name to the Sunday within the Octave of Christmas. The readings at Mass emphasize that God came to earth as a servant, submitted to the law of Moses and was offered in the temple, just as he was subject to his parents in their home at Nazareth. The example of the Holy Family is one of community sharing and loving (first passage here). Mary's sufferings begin when they lose Jesus on the road to Jerusalem and find him three days later in the temple, and the gospel (third passage here) reminds us of the further suffering Mary was to undergo at the foot of the cross.

Put on then, as God's chosen ones, holy and beloved, compassion, kindness, lowliness, meekness, and patience, forbearing one another and, if one has a complaint against another, forgiving each other; as the Lord has forgiven you, so you also must forgive. And above all these put on love, which binds everything together in perfect harmony. And let the peace of Christ rule in your hearts, to which indeed you were called in the one body. And be thankful. Let the word of Christ dwell in you richly, as you teach and admonish one another in all wisdom, and as you sing psalms and hymns and spiritual songs with thankfulness in your hearts to God. And whatever you do, in word or deed, do everything in the name of the Lord Jesus, giving thanks to God the Father through him.

Wives, be subject to your husbands, as is fitting in the Lord. Husbands, love your wives, and do not be harsh with them. Children, obey your parents in everything, for this pleases the Lord.

Colossians 3:12-20

And his father and his mother marvelled at what was said about him; and Simeon blessed them and said to Mary his mother,

"Behold, this child is set for the fall
        and rising of many in Israel,
and for a sign that is spoken against
(and a sword will pierce through your
        own soul also)
that thoughts out of many hearts may
        be revealed...."

And when they had performed everything according to the law of the Lord, they returned to Galilee, to their own city, Nazareth. And the child grew and became strong, filled with wisdom; and the favour of God was upon him.

Luke 2:33-5, 39-40

Now his parents went to Jerusalem every year at the feast of the Passover. And when he was twelve years old, they went up according to custom; and when the feast was ended, as they were returning, the boy Jesus stayed behind in Jerusalem. His parents did not know it, but supposing him to be in the company they went a day's journey, and they sought him among their kinsfolk and acquaintances; and when they did not find him, they returned to Jerusalem, seeking for him. After three days they found him in the temple, sitting among the teachers, listening to them and asking them questions; and all who heard him were amazed at his understanding and his answers. And when they saw him they were astonished; and his mother said to him, "Son, why have you treated us so? Behold, your father and I have been looking for you anxiously." And he said to them, "How is it that you sought me? Did you not know that I must be in my

35

Father's house?" And they did not understand the saying which he spoke to them. And he went down with them and came to Nazareth, and was obedient to them; and his mother kept all these things in her heart.

Luke 2:41-51

1 January
Solemnity of Mary, the Mother of God

"God sent his Son born of a woman. Mary is the Mother of Christ and the Mother of the Church. By the power of the Holy Spirit she is linked to God in a unique way. She is also our spiritual Mother who encourages us to say 'Yes' to God as our Father."

From the Roman Sunday Missal

The Second Vatican Council's Constitution on the Sacred Liturgy declared that feasts of the Blessed Virgin Mary were to be emphasized, for she "is joined by an inseparable bond to the saving work of her Son." Today's celebration replaces that of the Circumcision of the Lord and the Octave Day of Christmas. It is the most theological of the feasts of Mary throughout the year, recalling her dignity as Theotokos *(God-bearer), her most authoritative title, from which all her other privileges stem: "Mary was involved in the mysteries of Christ. As the most holy mother of God she was, after her Son, exalted by divine grace above all angels and men. Hence the Church appropriately honours her with special reverence. Indeed, from most ancient times the Blessed Virgin has been venerated under the title 'God-bearer'." (Dogmatic Constitution on the Church,* Lumen Gentium, *n. 66).*

That Mary is indeed "God-bearer" was defined at the Council of Ephesus in 431, after some early Fathers had championed a weaker term, Christotokos *(Christ-bearer), which was seen to threaten the doctrine of the unity between God and humanity in Christ. The Council of Ephesus was followed by a great outburst of devotion to Mary, with churches dedicated to her in all major cities. The doctrine was re-stated at the Council of Chalcedon in 451, where Christ was*

37

declared to be "true God and true man...born for us and for our salvation of Mary the Virgin and mother of God in his humanity." This has remained the faith of the Church ever since.

Adapted from Butler's Lives of the Saints,
January volume

PRAYER

O GOD, you bestowed on mankind the prize of everlasting salvation through the virginal motherhood of blessed Mary: let us be graced with her prayers, since through her we have received the giver of life, our Lord Jesus Christ your Son.

Collect, from The Layman's Missal and Prayer Book *(1962)*

PRAYERS OF SAINT FRANCIS OF ASSISI

HAIL, HOLY LADY, most Lady Queen, Mother of God,
O Mary who art forever virgin,
chosen by the most holy Father of heaven,
sanctified by him and his most holy and beloved Son
with the Holy Spirit, the Comforter,
you who were and shall remain
in the fullness of grace and all goodness!
Hail to the palace, tabernacle,
house, garments and handmaiden.
Hail, Mother of God!
And hail to all holy virtues, which,
through the grace and light of the Holy Spirit,
are poured into the hearts of the faithful,
and make us, who are unfaithful, faithful to God.

ALL POWERFUL,
most holy, most high and sovereign God;
sovereign goodness, universal goodness,
complete goodness;
you who alone are good: let us give you all praise,
all glory, all thanks, all honour, all blessing.

Trans. from Quatre petites prières de S. François d'Assise

At Compline, the antiphon Alma Redemptoris Mater *(see p.8) is said or sung, followed by*

℣. Post partum virgo inviolata permansisti.
℟. Dei Genitrix, intercede pro nobis.

Oremus:
DEUS, qui salutis aeternae, beatae Mariae virginitate foecunda, humano generi praemia praestitisti, tribue quaesumus, ut ipsam pro nobis intercedere sentiamus, per quam meruimus auctorem vitae suscipere, Dominum nostrum Jesum Christum Filium tuum. Amen.

℣. After childbirth thou didst remain a pure virgin.
℟. Intercede for us, O Mother of God.

Let us pray:
O God, who by the fruitful virginity of blessed Mary, hast given to mankind the rewards of eternal salvation; grant, we beseech thee, that we may experience her intercession for us, through whom we have deserved to receive the author of life, our Lord Jesus Christ thy Son.
May the divine assistance remain always with us. Amen

Eng. trans. from The Garden of the Soul, *compiled by Bishop Challoner (1691-1781) and often revised and reprinted*

HYMN: HOLY MARY, FULL OF GRACE

WHEN creation was begun,
God had chosen you to be
Mother of his blessed Son,
Holy Mary, full of grace.
Ave, Ave, Ave Maria.

When creation was restored,
You were there beside the Lord
Whom you cherished and adored,
Holy Mary, full of grace.
Ave, Ave, Ave Maria.

All of us are children too,
Often doubtful what to do,
Needing to confide in you,
Holy Mary, full of grace.
Ave, Ave, Ave Maria.

You are with us day by day
In our joys and our dismay:
Make us joyful as we say,
"Holy Mary, full of grace."
Ave, Ave, Ave Maria.

Lady, take us by surprise:
Dazzle our unseeing eyes,
Show us where true beauty lies,
Holy Mary, full of grace.
Ave, Ave, Ave Maria.

Lead us to your child above:
He will teach us how to love,

40

CHRISTMAS

How to pity and forgive,
Holy Mary, full of grace.
Ave, Ave, Ave Maria.

In the vision which transcends
All our dreams, and never ends,
God will gather all his friends
In the kingdom of your Son.
Ave, Ave, Ave Maria.

Praise the Father and the Son
And the Spirit, three in one,
As it was when time began,
Now and evermore. Amen.
Ave, Ave, Ave Maria.

J.-P. Lecot, trans. Michael Hodgetts

For Sundays during the Christmas period:

HYMN: O PUREST OF CREATURES
Maria Zu Lieben   *11 11.11 11*   *Paderborn Gesangbuch, 1765*

O PUREST of creatures! sweet Mother, sweet maid;
The one spotless womb wherein Jesus was laid.
Dark night has come down on us, Mother, and we
Look out for thy shining, sweet Star of the Sea.

Deep night hath come down on this rough-spoken world,
And the banners of darkness are boldly unfurled;
And the tempest-tossed Church—all her eyes are on thee:
They look to thy shining, sweet Star of the Sea.

Earth gave him one lodging; 'twas deep in thy breast,
And God found a home where the sinner finds rest;
His home and his hiding-place, both were in thee;
He was won by thy shining, sweet Star of the Sea.

Oh, blissful and calm was the wonderful rest
That thou gavest thy God in thy virginal breast;
For the heaven he left he found heaven in thee,
And he shone to thy shining, sweet Star of the Sea.

Frederick William Faber (1814-63)

For Our Lady's Saturdays

HYMN TO THE VIRGIN

OF one that is so fair and bright,
Velut maris stella;
Brighter than the day is light,
Parens et puella:
I cry to thee, thou see to me,
[I cry to thee to turn to me,]
Lady, pray thy Son for me,
Tam pia,
That I may come to thee,
Maria!

All this world was forlorn
Eva peccatrice,
Till our Lord was yborne
De te genetrice.
With *Ave* it went away

Darkest night, and comes the day
Salutis;
The well springeth out of thee,
Virtutis.

[In sorrow counsel thou art best,
Felix fecundata;
For all the weary thou art rest,
Mater honorata;
Beseech him in thy mildest mood,
Who for us did shed his blood,
In cruce,
That we may come to him,
In luce.]

Lady, flow'r of ev'rything,
Rosa sine spina,
Thou bore Jesu, heaven's King,
Gratia divina:
Of all pearls thou bear'st the prize
[of all I say thou bore the prize]
Lady queen of paradise
Electa:
Maiden mild, mother *es*
Effecta.

Anon., c. 1300 [= alternative medieval English version]

Hymn: O Mother Blest

St Ursula   *86.86.75.75*   *F. Westlake (1840-98)*

O Mother blest, whom God bestows
On sinners and on just,
What joy, what hope thou givest those
Who in thy mercy trust.

Thou art clement, thou art chaste,
Mary, thou art fair;
Of all mothers sweetest, best,
None with thee compare.

MAIDEN AND MOTHER

O heavenly Mother, mistress sweet!
It never yet was told
That suppliant sinner left thy feet
Unpitied, unconsoled.
Thou art clement...

O Mother, pitiful and mild,
Cease not to pray for me;
For I do love thee as a child,
And sigh for love of thee.
Thou art clement...

Most powerful Mother, all men know
Thy Son denies thee nought;
Thou askest, wishes it, and lo!
His power thy will hath wrought.
Thou art clement...

O Mother blest, for me obtain,
Ungrateful though I be,
To love that God who first could deign
To show such love for me.
Thou art clement...

Words by St Alphonsus de'Liguori (1696-1787)
Trans. E. Vaughan, C.SS.R. (1827-1908)

PRAYER TO OUR LADY

On the Sanctity of Human Life

Holy Virgin,
you experienced the sublime mystery of motherhood
as no other woman in the world.
While faith enabled you to welcome the Lord's Word,
your body made itself a fertile place for his incarnation.

O Mother,
accompany us toward an ever deeper perception
of the dignity of every human being.
Grant a clear awareness of it
especially to the men and women called to
the lofty vocation of parenthood,
so that they may always be "sanctuaries of life"
through the miracle of giving birth,
entrusted by God
to the authenticity of their faithful love
and watchful responsibility.
Amen.

Pope John Paul II, delivered in St Peter's Piazza,
Sunday, 19 December 1993

2 February
The Presentation of the Lord

This feast was observed in Jerusalem as early as the fourth century, as the Hypapante, *meaning "meeting," as it recalled the encounter between the child Jesus and Simeon in the temple described in Luke 2:25ff (see next page). It was first observed on 14 February, forty days after what was then the Nativity on 6 January; when the Nativity was fixed on 25 December, it was put back to 2 February. Jewish law prescribed that parents should make an offering in the temple forty days after the birth of a male child, and Mary and Joseph made the offering of poor people, two turtle-doves. The mother was then declared ritually pure after childbirth. The name "Purification" first replaced "Presentation" in France around the eighth century and gradually took hold elsewhere. The practice of blessing candles on this day, which gives it its alternative name of Candlemas, stems from the early practice of carrying lights in the liturgical procession, which was originally an act of atonement for pagan practices. In Rome in the Middle Ages the procession took place in darkness from the church of St Adrian, in which the candles were blessed, to the basilica of St Mary Major.*

The Presentation of Our Lady in the temple, celebrated on 21 November (see p. 200) refers to her supposed dedication to temple service by her parents, not to this gospel episode.

FIRST ANTIPHON AT THE PROCESSION
(Said or sung from the Presentation to Maundy Thursday)

ADORNA thalamum tuum, Sion,
et suspice Regem Christum:
amplectere Mariam, quae est caelestis porta:
ipsa enim portat Regem gloriae novi luminis:
subsistit Virgo, adducens manibus
Filium ante luciferum genitum:
quem accipiens Simeon in ulnas suas,
praedicavit populis
Dominum eum esse vitae et mortis
et Salvatorem mundi.

Sion, adorn your bridal bower
and welcome Mary with open arms,
for she it is who brings us heaven.
She comes bringing our new light, the King of Glory.
She stands there, a virgin, holding in her hands
and offering her Son,
born before the day-star was created.
And Simeon takes the child in his arms
and proclaims to all the people
that this is the Lord of life and death,
the Saviour of the world.

GOSPEL READING

Now there was a man in Jerusalem, whose name was Simeon, and this man was righteous and devout, looking for the consolation of Israel, and the Holy Spirit was upon him. And it had been revealed to him by the Holy Spirit that he should not see death before he had seen the Lord's Christ. And inspired by the Spirit he came into the temple; and when the parents brought in the child Jesus,

49

to do for him according to the custom of the law, he took him up in his arms and blessed God and said,

    "Lord, now lettest thou thy servant
        depart in peace,
    according to thy word;
    for mine eyes have seen thy salvation
    which thou hast prepared in the
        presence of all peoples,
    a light for revelation to the Gentiles
    and for glory to thy people Israel."

And his father and mother marvelled at what was said about him; and Simeon blessed them and said to Mary his mother, "This child is set for the fall and rising of many in Israel (and a sword will pierce through your own soul also), that thoughts out of many hearts may be revealed."

Luke 2:25-35

HYMN: THE PRESENTATION

Maria Jung und Zart   66.66.   *Psalteriolum Harmonicum (1642)*

    They say it is a king
    His temple entering;
    His temple doth not rock
    With gust and earthquake shock.

But all the air is stilled,
As at a law fulfilled;
Mary, to keep God's word,
Brings babe and turtle-bird.

Lo, Simeon draweth in,
And doth his song begin;
Great doom is for her Son,
And Mary's heart undone.

Oh, Simeon is blessed;
Christ in his arms is pressed;
Mary's sweet doves are slain;
She takes her babe again.

And in her heart she knows
He will be slain, as those;
And on her journey home
She feels God's kingdom come.

Michael Field

HYMN: REFULSIT ALMAE DIES LUCIS CANDIDUS

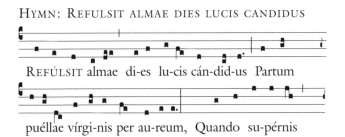

REFÚLSIT almae di-es lu-cis cán-did-us Partum

puéllae vírgi-nis per au-reum, Quando su-pérnis

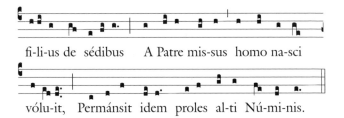

fi-li-us de sédibus   A Patre mis-sus homo na-sci

vólu-it, Permánsit idem proles al-ti Nú-mi-nis.

Legis sacratae sanctis ceremoniis
Subjectus omnis calamo Mosaico
Dignatur esse, qui regit perfulgidos
In arce Patris ordines angelicos
Caelum, qui terram fundavit ac maria.

Postquam puellae dies quadragesimus
Est adimpletus juxta legem Domini,
Maria virgo Jesum sanctum puerum
Ulnis sacratis templi tunc in atriis
Tulit, tremendi genitoris unicum.

Mater beata carnis sub velamine
Deum ferebat humeris castissimis,
Dulcia strictis basia sub labiis,
Deoque vero homini impresserat,
Ore jubente quo sunt cuncta condita.

Duos parentes tulerunt candidulos
Pullos columbae lacteolis plumulis,
Dedere templo par pro eo turturum,
Veluti legis promulgabat sanctio,
Quales perustas consecrarent hostias.

From the Breviary of the monastery of St Severinus, Naples (first five verses)

ORDINARY TIME BEFORE LENT

The golden dawn hath brought the light of that blest day
Adorned with the childbearing of a virgin fair,
When God descended from his throne on high
Sent from the Father, and in flesh willed to be born,
Remaining still the Sole-begotten of the Lord.

And here on earth for us he deigned to undergo
The holy rites commanded by the ancient law
Writ by the hand of Moses, though he rules on high
The shining hosts of angels in his Father's land
And built the earth and sea and sky and all the stars.

And knowing now the mystic forty days were past
Ordained of old by the commandment of the Lord,
Mary the mother-maid took up the holy child
Who ever with the Founder of the world is one,
And bore him in her arms unto the temple halls.

The blessed Mother nestling bare against her breast
The God who made her and upheld her, veiled in flesh,
And looking down on him who is both God and man
She kissed with the sweet kisses of her mouth his lips,
Those lips that spake of old time, and the worlds were made.

And the two parents brought before the Lord of Hosts
Two pigeons clothed in plumage soft and white as milk,
And in the temple gave a pair of turtledoves
That should be consecrate as a burnt sacrifice,
As had of old been writ and sanctioned by the Law.

Trans. Alan G. McDougall (dates unknown),
published in Pange Lingua *(1916)*

HYMN: WHEN TO THE TEMPLE MARY WENT

When to the temple Mary went,
And brought the Holy Child,
Him did the aged Simeon see,
As it had been revealed.

He took up Jesus in his arms
And blessing God, he said:
"In peace I now depart
My Saviour having seen,
The hope of Israel,
The light of men."

Help now thy servants, gracious Lord,
That we may ever be,
As once the faithful Simeon was,
rejoicing but in thee:

And when we must from
Earth departure take,
may we gently fall asleep,
And with thee awake.

Johannes Eccard (1553-1611)

From the Presentation of the Lord to Maundy Thursday

COMPLINE ANTIPHON: AVE REGINA CAELORUM

Solesmes Plainsong

A-ve Re-gí-na cae-ló-rum,   Ave Dómi-na

ange-ló-rum Salve ra-dix, salve, porta, Ex qua

mundo lux est orta: Gaude, Virgo glo-ri-ó-sa,

Su-per omnes spe-ci-ó-sa: Va-le, O valde de-có-ra

Et pro no-bis Christum exó-ra.

℣. Dignare me laudare te, Virgo sacrata.
℟. Da mihi virtutem contra hostes tuos.

Oremus:
CONCEDE, misericors Deus, fragilitati nostrae praesidium; ut qui sanctae Dei Genitricis memoriam agimus,
intercessionis ejus auxilio a nostris iniquitatibus resurga-
mus. Per eundem Christum Dominum nostrum. Amen.

MAIDEN AND MOTHER

Hail, O Queen of heaven enthron'd!
Hail, by angels mistress own'd!
Root of Jesse, gate of morn,
Whence the world's true Light was born.
Glorious Virgin, joy to thee,
Loveliest whom in heaven they see.
Fairest thou where all are fair!
Plead with Christ our sins to spare.

℣. *Vouchsafe that I may praise thee, O sacred Virgin.*
℟. *Give me strength against thine enemies.*

Let us pray:
Comfort most merciful God, the frailty of our hearts with thy
protection; that as we do keep the holy Mother of God in our
remembrance, the power of her intercession may raise us up
from all our iniquities. Through the same Christ our Lord.
Amen.

11 February
Our Lady of Lourdes

On 11 February 1858 a fourteen-year-old girl named Marie-Bernarde (known as Bernadette) Soubirous was walking home with two companions from Bartrès, two miles north of the town of Lourdes on the northern slopes of the Pyrenees in south-western France. In a cave beside the River Gave, a natural cavity in the rock-face known as Massabielle, she saw a vision she described as "Something white in the form of an extraordinarily beautiful young girl, not as tall as Bernadette [she was 4' 7"], in a white dress gathered at the waist with a blue ribbon. She had a white veil on her head with her hair showing at the temples, a yellow rose on each foot, leaving only her toes showing, and a rosary in her hand." The vision corresponded to popular representations of the Immaculate Conception.

From that date to 16 July, Bernadette experienced a total of eighteen separate apparitions. The "Lady" asked her to say the Rosary with her and promised to make her "happy [not] in this world but in the next," asked her to do penance and pray for sinners, and told her to drink from a spring. There was no spring in the cave, but the next day Bernadette scratched at the soil, and muddy water began to ooze out, soon turning into a clear stream, which has been flowing ever since. Bernadette was told to "tell the priests that people should come here in procession and build a chapel here." Finally, speaking in the local dialect, she told Bernadette who she was: "Que soy era Immaculada Conceptiou" — "I am the Immaculate Conception." Despite clerical scepticism, the shrine soon became popular and, helped by the building of railways, developed into and has remained the greatest Marian place of pilgrimage in the world. The sick come in great numbers from all over the world, and many remarkable cures have been recorded. All who take part in the pilgrimages return spiritually refreshed with their faith and hope reaffirmed through an exercise in communal charity that would be hard to find paralleled anywhere else.

Bernadette herself withdrew from the limelight and became a nun at Nevers, where she died in 1879 at the age of only thirty-five. She was canonized in 1933, and her feast is celebrated on 16 April.

PRAYER TO OUR LADY OF LOURDES

O IMMACULATE Virgin Mary,
 you are the refuge of sinners,
 the health of the sick,
 and the comfort of the afflicted.
By your appearances at the grotto of Lourdes
 you made it a privileged sanctuary
 where your favours are given to people
 streaming to it from the whole world.
Over the years countless sufferers
 have obtained the cure of their infirmities,
 whether of soul, mind, or body.
Therefore I come with limitless confidence
 to implore your motherly intercessions.
Loving Mother,
 obtain the grant of my requests.
Let me strive to imitate your virtues on earth
so that I may one day share your glory in heaven.

COLLECT

DEUS, qui per immaculatam Virginis conceptionem dignum Filio tuo habitaculum praeparasti: supplices a te

quaesumus; ut ejusdem Virginis apparitionem celebrantes, salutem mentis et corporis consequamur.
*O God, in the Virgin's immaculate conception you made
ready a dwelling-place fit for your Son. We humbly pray that
we who celebrate the appearing of that Virgin may be given
health of mind and body.*

Layman's Missal and Prayer Book (1962)

LORD OF MERCY, as we keep the memory of Mary, the
immaculate Mother of God, who appeared to Bernadette
at Lourdes: grant us through her prayer strength in our
weakness and grace to rise up from our sins.

Roman Breviary

LOURDES HYMN: THE BELLS OF THE ANGELUS

> THE bells of the Angelus
> Call us to pray
> In sweet tones announcing
> The sacred Ave.
> *Ave, Ave, Ave Maria;*
> *Ave, Ave, Ave, Maria.*
>
> An angel of mercy
> Led Bernadette's feet
> Where flows the deep torrent
> Our Lady to greet.
> *Ave, Ave...*
>
> She prayed to our Mother
> That God's will be done,
> She prayed for his glory
> That his kingdom come.
> *Ave, Ave....*

Immaculate Mary,
Your praises we sing
Who reign now with Christ,
Our redeemer and king.
Ave, Ave…

In heaven the blessed
Your glory proclaim,
On earth now your children
Invoke your fair name.
Ave, Ave…

Words: author unknown   Melody: traditional French

Our Lady's Saturdays

THE LITANY OF
THE BLESSED VIRGIN

Solesmes Plainsong

Kyri-e e-lé-i-son.*ij.* Chríste e-lé-i-son.*ij.* Kyri-e e-lé-i-son

Chríste áudi nos. *ij.*   Chríste exáudi nos. *ij.*

Pá- ter   de caé-lis Dé-us,   mi-se-rére nóbis.
Fíli Redémptor mún-di Dé-us,   mi-se-rére nóbis.
Spí- ri- tus Sáncte Dé-us,   mi-se-rére nóbis.
Sán- cta Trínitas ú-nus Dé-us,   mi-se-rére nóbis.

Sán- cta Ma-rí- a,   óra pro nóbis

Sancta   Dé- i Gé- ni- trix   *óra pro nóbis*

Sancta   Vir- go vír- gi- num
          Má- ter Chrí- sti
Máter di- ví- nae grá- ti- ae
Má-   ter pu- rís- si- ma
Má-   ter ca- stís-si- sma
Máter in- vi- o- lá-   ta
Máter in- te- me- rá-   ta
Máter   ad- mi- rá- bi- lis
Máter bó- ni con- sí- li- i
Máter   Cre- a- tó-   ris
Máter   Sal- va- tó-   ris
Vírgo   pru-den- tís- si- ma
Vírgo   ve- ne- rán-   da
Vírgo   prae-di- cán-   da
          Vír- go pot- ens
          Ví-   go clé- mens
Vir-   go fi- dé- lis
Spécu-   lum ju- stí- ti- ae
Sédes   sa- pi- én- ti- ae
Cáusa nó- strae lae- tí- ti- ae
Vas spi- ri- tu- á-   le
Vas   ho- no- rá- bi- le

61

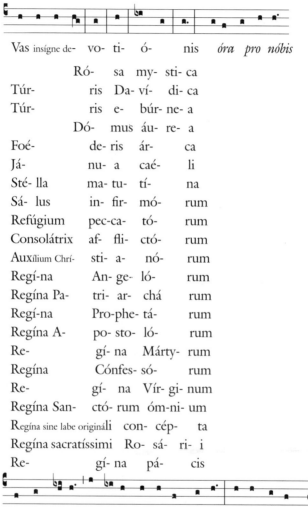

Vas insígne de- vo- ti- ó- nis *óra pro nóbis*

Ró- sa my- sti- ca

Túr- ris Da- ví- di- ca

Túr- ris e- búr- ne- a

Dó- mus áu- re- a

Foé- de- ris ár- ca

Já- nu- a caé- li

Sté- lla ma- tu- tí- na

Sá- lus in- fir- mó- rum

Refúgium pec-ca- tó- rum

Consolátrix af- fli- ctó- rum

Auxílium Chrí- sti- a- nó- rum

Regí-na An- ge- ló- rum

Regína Pa- tri- ar- chá rum

Regí-na Pro-phe- tá- rum

Regína A- po- sto- ló- rum

Re- gí- na Márty- rum

Regína Cónfes- só- rum

Re- gí- na Vír- gi- num

Regína San- ctó- rum óm-ni- um

Regína sine labe origináli con- cép- ta

Regína sacratíssimi Ro- sá- ri- i

Re- gí- na pá- cis

Agnus Dé-i, qui tóllis peccá-ta múndi, párce nóbis

Dó-mine.   Agnus Dé-i, qui tóllis peccá-ta múndi,

exáudi nos Dómine.   Agnus Dé-i,   qui tóllis

peccá-ta múndi,   mi-se-rére- nó-bis.

℣. Ora pro nobis, sancta Dei Genitrix.
℟. Ut digni efficiamur promissionibus Christi.
Oremus:
CONCEDE nos famulos tuos, quaesumus, Domine Deus,
perpertua mentis et corporis sanitate gaudere: et gloriosa
beatae Mariae semper virginis intercessione, a praesenti
liberari tristitia, et aeterna perfrui laetitia. Per Christum
Dominum nostrum. Amen.

THE LITANY OF THE BLESSED VIRGIN
IN ENGLISH

("Pray for us" is repeated after each invocation of Our Lady.)

Lord have mercy   *Lord have mercy*
Christ have mercy   *Christ have mercy*
Lord have mercy   *Lord have mercy*
Christ hear us   *Christ graciously hear us*

God the Father of heaven
Have mercy on us
God the Son, Redeemer of the world
Have mercy on us
God the Holy Spirit
Have mercy on us
Holy Trinity, one God
Have mercy on us

Holy Mary   *Pray for us*
Holy Mother of God
Holy Virgin of virgins
Mother of Christ
Mother of divine grace
Mother most pure
Mother most chaste
Mother inviolate
Mother undefiled
Mother most lovable
Mother most admirable
Mother of good counsel
Mother of our Creator
Mother of our Saviour
Virgin most prudent
Virgin most venerable
Virgin most renowned
Virgin most powerful
Virgin most merciful
Virgin most faithful
Mirror of justice
Seat of wisdom
Cause of our joy

Spiritual vessel
Vessel of honour
Singular vessel of devotion
Mystical rose
Tower of David
Tower of ivory
House of gold
Ark of the covenant
Gate of heaven
Morning star
Health of the sick
Refuge of sinners
Comfort of the afflicted
Help of Christians
Queen of Angels
Queen of Patriarchs
Queen of Prophets
Queen of Apostles
Queen of Martyrs
Queen of Confessors
Queen of Virgins
Queen of all Saints
Queen conceived without original sin
Queen assumed into heaven
Queen of the most holy Rosary
Queen of Peace
Lamb of God, you take away the sins of the world:
Spare us, O Lord.
Lamb of God, you take away the sins of the world:
Graciously hear us, O Lord.
Lamb of God, you take away the sins of the world:
Have mercy on us.

Pray for us, O holy Mother of God,
That we may be made worthy of the promises of Christ.

Let us pray:
LORD GOD, give to your people the joy of continual health in mind and body. With the prayers of the Virgin Mary to help us, guide us through the sorrows of this life to eternal happiness in the life to come. Grant this through our Lord, Jesus Christ, your Son, who lives and reigns with you and the Holy Spirit, one God, for ever and ever. Amen.

Otherwise known as the Litany of Loreto, this, the most popular of all litanies, appears to have been first printed in 1551, though an earlier and much longer version is known.

LENT AND EASTER

The Lenten period lasts from Ash Wednesday
to the end of Holy Saturday, excluding Sundays.
It is a period of fasting and penance
and its liturgical colour is purple, denoting sorrow for sin.

The feast of the Annunciation of the Lord,
25 March, usually occurs in Lent.

Easter is a time of rejoicing
and its liturgical colour is white, denoting rejoicing.

The month of May, devoted to Our Lady,
is usually divided between
the period following Easter and Pentecost.
May devotions are here included in the following section.

THE ANNUNCIATION
(See pages 75–8. Based on The Prayerbook of Margarete von Rodemachern)

Ash Wednesday

REMEMBER, O most gracious Virgin Mary, that never was it known that anyone who fled to thy protection, implored thy help and sought thy intercession, was left unaided. Inspired with this confidence, I fly unto thee, O Virgin of virgins, my Mother. To thee I come, before thee I stand, sinful and sorrowful. O Mother of the Word incarnate, despise not my petitions but in thy mercy hear and answer me. Amen.

St Bernard of Clairvaux (1090-1153)

During Lent

HYMN: STABAT MATER *AT THE CROSS*

Traditionally sung at the Stations of the Cross, three lines at a time while moving from one Station to the next

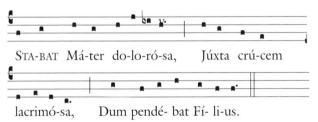

STA-BAT Má-ter do-lo-ró-sa,   Júxta crú-cem lacrimó-sa,   Dum pendé- bat Fí- li-us.

Cujus animam gementem,
Contristatam, et dolentem,
Pertransivit gladius.

O quam tristis et afflicta
Fuit illa benedicta
Mater unigeniti!

Quae moerebat et dolebat;
Pia Mater, dum videbat
Nati poenas inclyti.

Quis est homo qui non fleret,
Matrem Christi si videret
In tanto supplicio?

Quis non posset contristari
Christi Matrem contemplari
Dolentem cum Filio?

Pro peccatis suae gentis
Vidit Jesum in tormentis,
Et flagellis subditum.

Vidit suum dulcem Natum
Moriendo desolatum,
Dum emisit spiritum.

Eia Mater, fons amoris,
Me sentire vim doloris
Fac, ut tecum lugeam.

Fac ut ardeat cor meum
In amando Christum Deum
Ut sibi complaceam.

Sancta Mater, istud agas,
Crucifixi fige plagas
Cordi meo valide.

Tui nati vulnerati,
Tam dignati pro me pati,
Poenas mecum divide.

Fac me tecum pie flere,
Crucifixo condolere,
Donec ego vixero.

Juxta crucem tecum stare,
Et me tibi sociare
In planctu desidero.

Attributed to Jacopone da Todi (c. 1230-1306)

There are three further verses, not generally used. The usual musical setting is adapted by Dom A. Gregory Murray from a later form from the Mainzisch Gesangbuch *of 1661. Other settings have been made by Orlando de Lassus (1532-94); Giovanni Pierluigi da Palestrina (1525?-94); Giovanni Battista Pergolesi (1710-36); Franz Schubert (1797-1828); Giuseppe Verdi (1813-1901); Antonín Dvořák (1841-1904). Some words vary in different settings.*

At the cross her station keeping,
Stood the mournful Mother weeping,
Close to Jesus to the last;

Through her heart, his sorrow sharing,
All his bitter anguish bearing,
Now at length the sword has pass'd.

Oh, how sad and sore distress'd
Was that Mother highly blest
Of the sole-begotten One.

71

MAIDEN AND MOTHER

Christ above in torment hangs;
She beneath beholds the pangs
Of her dying glorious son.

Is there one who would not weep,
Whelm'd in miseries so deep,
Christ's dear Mother to behold?

Can the human heart refrain
From partaking in her pain,
In that Mother's pain untold?

Bruised, derided, cursed, defilèd,
She beheld her tender child,
All with bloody scourges rent;

For the sins of his own nation,
Saw him hang in desolation,
Till his spirit forth he sent.

O thou Mother! Fount of love!
Touch my spirit from above,
Make my heart with thine accord;

Make me feel as thou hast felt;
Make my soul to glow and melt
With the love of Christ my Lord.

Holy Mother, pierce me through,
In my heart each wound renew
Of my Saviour crucified.

Let me share with thee his pain
Who for all my sins was slain,
Who for me in torments died.

Let me mingle tears with thee,
Mourning him who mourned for me,
All the days that I may live;

By the cross with thee to stay,
There with thee to weep and pray,
Is all I ask of thee to give.

Trans. Edward Caswall (1814-78)

At the Fourth Station of the Cross
Consider the meeting of the Son and the Mother, which took
place on this journey. Their looks became like so many arrows
to wound those hearts which loved each other so tenderly.

Still burdened with his cross, and wounded yet more by
his fall, Jesus proceeds on his way. He is met by his
Mother. What a meeting must that have been! What a
sword of anguish must have pierced that Mother's
bosom! What must have been the compassion of that
Son for his holy Mother!

O JESUS, by the compassion which thou didst feel for
thy Mother, have compassion on us, and give us a share
in her intercession. O Mary, most afflicted Mother, intercede for us, that by the sufferings of thy Son we may be
delivered from the wrath to come.

At the Thirteenth Station of the Cross
Consider how after Our Lord had expired two of his disciples,
Joseph and Nicodemus, took him down from the cross and
placed him in the arms of his afflicted Mother, who received
him with unutterable tenderness and pressed him to her
breast.

The multitude have left the heights of Calvary, and none remain save the beloved disciple and the holy women who, at the foot of the cross, are striving to stem the grief of Christ's inconsolable Mother. Joseph of Arimathea and Nicodemus take down the body of her divine Son from the cross and deposit it in her arms.

O THOU, whose grief was boundless as an ocean that hath no limits, Mary, Mother of God, give us a share in thy most holy sorrow in the sufferings of thy Son, and have compassion on our infirmities. Accept us as thy children with the beloved disciple. Shew thyself a mother unto us; and may he, through thee, receive our prayer, who for us vouchsafed to be thy Son.

Two meditations and prayers from a traditional English version of the Stations of the Cross, recommended by Cardinal Nicholas Wiseman to the faithful in 1850

A PRAYER *In suffering, to Mary the Mother of Jesus*

O HOLY Virgin, in the midst of your days of glory do not forget the sorrows of this earth. Cast a merciful glance upon those who are suffering, struggling against difficulties, their lips constantly pressed against life's bitter cup. Have pity on those who love each other and are separated, have pity on our rebellious hearts, have pity on our weak faith, have pity on those we love. Have pity on those who weep, on those who pray, on those who fear. Grant hope and peace to all. Amen.

25 March
The Annunciation

THE ANGELUS

The angel of the Lord declared unto Mary,
And she conceived by the Holy Spirit;

Hail Mary...
Holy Mary...

Behold the handmaid of the Lord:
Be it done unto me according to your word;

Hail Mary...
Holy Mary...

And the Word was made flesh
And dwelt amongst us;

Hail Mary...
Holy Mary...

Pray for us, O Holy Mother of God,
That we may be made worthy of the promises of Christ.

Let us pray:
POUR forth, we beseech you O Lord, your grace into our
hearts, that we, to whom the incarnation of Christ, your
Son, was made known by the message of an angel, may,
by his passion and cross, be brought to the glory of his
resurrection, through Christ, our Lord. Amen

❧

NOVENA PRAYER

O MOST holy Virgin, who was chosen by the adorable Trinity from all eternity to be the most pure Mother of Jesus; permit us, thy devoted children, to remind thee of the joy thou didst receive in the instant of the most sacred incarnation of our divine Lord, and during the nine months thou didst carry him in thy chaste womb. We salute thee, O ever-blessèd Virgin Mother of God, abyss of grace, and miracle of almighty power. We salute thee, O sanctuary of the most holy Trinity, Queen of the universe, and Refuge of sinners. We salute thee, O ever-faithful Virgin, Mirror of sanctity, Mother of mercy, and our Mother. Attracted by thy maternal tenderness, and confiding in thy never-failing mediation, we cast ourselves at thy feet, and implore of thee to obtain for us, of thy dear Son, the grant of the favour we ask in this Novena... Vouchsafe to hear our sighs, and reject not our petitions, O pure and immaculate Mother; obtain for us purity of soul and body, a constant love of God, and a perfect obedience to his most holy will, that, living but for him here, we may love and enjoy him hereafter with thee, for ever and ever. Amen.

Recited in choir after vespers from the 16th to the 25th of March

COLLECT

DEUS, qui de beatae Mariae Virginis utero Verbum tuum, angelo nuntiante, carnem suscipere voluisti: praesta supplicibus tuis: ut, qui vere eam Genitricem Dei credimus, ejus apud te intercessionibus adjuvemur.

O God, you willed that your Word should take flesh in the Blessed Virgin Mary's womb at the message of an angel, and we know that she is indeed the Mother of God: grant that we your suppliants may be helped by her intercession with you.

GOSPEL READING

In the sixth month the angel Gabriel was sent from God to a city of Galilee named Nazareth, to a virgin betrothed to a man whose name was Joseph, of the house of David; and the virgin's name was Mary. And he came to her and said, "Hail, full of grace, the Lord is with you!" But she was greatly troubled at the saying, and considered in her mind what sort of greeting this might be. And the angel said to her, "Do not be afraid, Mary, for you have found favour with God. And behold, you will conceive in your womb and bear a son, and you shall call his name Jesus.

He will be great, and will be called the
Son of the Most High;
and the Lord God will give to him the
throne of his father David,
and he will reign over the house of Jacob for ever;
and of his kingdom there will be no end."

And Mary said to the angel, "How can this be, since I have no husband?" And the angel said to her,

"The Holy Spirit will come upon you,
and the power of the Most High will
overshadow you;
therefore the child to be born will be called holy,
the Son of God.

And behold, your kinswoman Elizabeth in her old age has also conceived a son, and this is the sixth month with her who was called barren. For with God nothing will be impossible." And Mary said, "Behold, I am the handmaid of the Lord; let it be to me according to your word." And the angel departed from her.

Luke 1:26-38

HYMN

THE angel Gabriel from heaven came.
His wings as drifted snow, his eyes as flame.
"All hail," said he, "Thou lowly maiden, Mary,
Most highly favoured lady!"
Gloria!

"For know, a blessèd Mother thou shalt be.
All generations laud and honour thee.
Thy Son shall be Emmanuel, by seers foretold,
Most highly favoured lady!"
Gloria!

Then gentle Mary meekly bowed her head.
"To me be, as it pleaseth God," she said,
"My soul shall laud and magnify his holy name,
Most highly favoured lady!"
Gloria!

Of her, Emmanuel, the Christ, was born
In Bethlehem, all on a Christmas morn;
And Christian folk throughout the world will ever say:
"Most highly favoured lady!"
Gloria!

Sabine Baring Gould (1834-1924)

AVE MARIA

AVE MARIA, gratia plena,
Dominus tecum,
Benedicta tu in mulieribus,
et benedictus fructus ventris tui. Amen.

The first part of the more familiar Ave Maria *is set to music*
by Robert Parsons (c. 1530-70)

Good Friday

HYMN: *Mother of Mercy, Day by Day*
(Repeat the last line of each verse)

MOTHER of Mercy, day by day
My love of thee grows more and more;
Thy gifts are strewn upon my way,
Like sands upon the great seashore.

Though poverty and work and woe
The masters of my life may be,
When times are worst, who does not know
Darkness is light with love of thee?

But scornful men have coldly said
Thy love was leading me from God;
And yet in this I did but tread
The very path my Saviour trod.

They know but little of thy worth
Who speak these heartless words to me;
For what did Jesus love on earth
One half so tenderly as thee?

Get me the grace to love thee more;
Jesus will give if thou wilt plead;
And, Mother! when life's cares are o'er,
Oh, I shall love thee then indeed!

Jesus, when his three hours were run,
Bequeath'd thee from the cross to me,
And oh! how can I love thy Son,
Sweet Mother! if I love not thee?

Frederick William Faber (1814-63)

PRAYER BEFORE THE CROSS ON GOOD FRIDAY

O LADY blest, Sweet Virgin, hear my cry:
Forgive the wrong that I have done
To thee, in causing thy dear Son
Upon the cross to die.

The last verse of the hymn "Sleep, holy Babe"
by Edward Caswall (1814-78)

Easter

ANTIPHON: REGINA CAELI LAETARE

From compline on Holy Saturday to first vespers of Trinity Sunday

REGI-NA cae-li lae-tá-re,   alle-lú-ia:

Qui-a quem mer-u-ísti portáre,   alle-lú-ia:

Re-surréxit, sic-ut di-xit,   alle-lú-ia

O-ra pro no-bis De-um,   alle-lú- ia.

℣. Gaude et laetare, Virgo Maria, alleluia.
℞. Quia surrexit Dominus vere, alleluia.

Oremus:
DEUS qui per resurrectionem Filii tui Domini nostri Jesus Christi mundum laetificare dignatus es; praesta, quaesumus, ut per ejus Genitricem Virginem Mariam perpetuae capiamus guadia vitae. Per eundem Christum Dominum nostrum. Amen.

> *Rejoice, O Queen of heaven, alleluia,*
> *for he whom thou didst merit to bear, alleluia,*
> *has risen as he said, alleluia.*
> *Pray for us to God, alleluia.*

℣. *Rejoice and be glad, O Virgin Mary, alleluia*
℞. *For the Lord has risen indeed, alleluia.*

Let us pray:
O God, who didst vouchsafe to give joy to the world through the resurrection of thy Son, our Lord Jesus Christ; grant, we beseech thee, that through his Mother, the Virgin Mary, we may obtain the joys of everlasting life. Through the same Christ our Lord. Amen.

AVE VERUM   *Ascribed to Pope Innocent VI (d. 1362*

Ave Verum   *Irreg.*   A.G.M.

AVE verum corpus, natum
Ex Maria Virgine,
Vere passum, immolatum
In cruce pro homine.
Cujus latus perforatum
Vero fluxit sanguine;
Esto nobis praegustatum,
Mortis in examine.
O clemens,
O pie,
O dulcis Jesu,
Fili Mariae.

82

Hail true body,
born of the Virgin Mary,
that truly suffered and was sacrificed
on the cross for our sake
From whose pierced side
' *blood truly flowed.*
Become for us a foretaste
of our own death.
O kind,
O loving,
O sweet Jesu,
Son of Mary.

Another musical setting is by Sir Edward Elgar (1857-1934),
his Opus 2/1 (1887).

❧

PRAYER OF ST CYRIL

HAIL, Mother and Virgin,
  living and immortal tabernacle of God,
  the world's treasure and light,
  ornament of virgins, support of true faith,
  firm foundation of every church.
  Thou who gavest birth to God,
  and carried under thy pure heart Him
  whom space cannot contain.
  Thou through whom the Holy Trinity is praised
  and worshipped and through whom the
  holy cross is venerated in the whole world.

St Cyril, Patriarch of Alexandria and Doctor of the Church (c.376-444)
May be said from the 2nd to the 6th Sunday of Easter

PENTECOST

*The feast of Pentecost (or Whit Sunday) is celebrated
on the eighth Sunday after Easter.
The first Sunday after Pentecost is Trinity Sunday.*

*The month of May is devoted to the Blessed Virgin Mary
and known as "Our Lady's Month." It culminates in the
feast of the Visitation of the Blessed Virgin Mary on the 31st.*

*The Immaculate Heart of Mary
is now celebrated as an obligatory Memorial
on the Saturday following the Second Sunday
after Pentecost*

*Showing devotion to Mary in the month of May probably
reflects an attempt to "Christianize" spring festivals.
The practice seems to have originated in Spain
during the thirteenth century.
May devotions became common, though as private devotions,
in the sixteenth century, with praying of the rosary
and saying the litany of Loreto.
From the mid-eighteenth century the custom spread
as a public devotion throughout the world.*

*The liturgical colour for Pentecost Sunday
(and its Vigil Mass) is red,
signifying the tongues of fire
in which the Holy Spirit came down upon the apostles.*

85

THE VISITATION
*(see pages 106–111. Based on The Prayerbook of
Margarete von Rodemachern)*

May – Our Lady's Month

(The prayers and hymns for different times of day are from the Little Office of The Immaculate Conception of The Blessed Virgin. The translation is slightly modernized from that of The Golden Manual *published in 1850, made from the text promulgated in Rome in 1838.)*

At Dawn (Matins)

> *Come, my lips, and wide proclaim*
> *The Blessed Virgin's spotless fame.*

> O Lady, make speed to befriend me,
> from the hands of the enemy mightily defend me.

> Glory be to the Father, and to the Son
> and to the Holy Spirit. Amen. Alleluia.

HYMN

> HAIL, Queen of the heavens,
> Hail, Mistress of earth.
> Hail, Virgin most pure,
> Of immaculate birth.

87

Clear Star of the morning
In beauty enshrined,
O Lady, make speed
To the help of mankind.

You, God in the depth
Of eternity chose,
And formed you all fair
As his glorious spouse.

And called you his Word's
Own Mother to be,
By whom he created
The earth, sky, and sea. Amen.

God elected her, and pre-elected her,
He made her to dwell in his tabernacle.

O Lady, hear my prayer,
and let my cry come unto you.

Let us pray:
Holy Mary, Queen of heaven, Mother of our Lord Jesus
Christ and of his Church, who forsakes no one and
despises no one, look upon me with an eye of pity, and
entreat for me of your beloved Son the forgiveness of all
my sins; that, as I now celebrate with affection your holy
and immaculate conception, so hereafter, I may receive
the prize of eternal blessedness, by the grace of him
whom you, in virginity, brought forth, Jesus Christ our
Lord: who, with the Father and the holy Spirit, lives and
reigns, in perfect Trinity, God for ever and ever. Amen.

O Lady, hear my prayer,
and let my cry come unto you.

Let us bless the Lord.
Thanks be to God.

May the souls of the faithful departed, through
the mercy of God, rest in peace. Amen.

❧

In the Morning (Prime)
O Lady, make speed to befriend me,
from the hands of the enemy mightily defend me.
Glory be…Alleluia.

HYMN

HAIL, Virgin most wise,
Hail, deity's shrine
With seven fair pillars
And table divine.

Preserved from the guilt
Which has come on us all,
Exempt in the womb
From the taint of the fall.

O new star of Jacob,
Of angels the Queen,
O gate of the saints,
O mother of men.

O terrible as
The embattled array,
Be you of the faithful
The refuge and stay. Amen.

The Lord himself created her in the Holy Spirit,
and poured her out among all his works.

O Lady, hear my prayer,
and let my cry come unto you.

Let us bless the Lord.
Thanks be to God.

May the souls of the faithful departed,
through the mercy of God, rest in peace. Amen.

✣

At Mid-Morning (Terce)

O Lady, make speed to befriend me,
from the hands of the enemy mightily defend me.
Glory be… Alleluia.

HYMN

HAIL, Solomon's throne,
Pure ark of the law,
Fair rainbow and bush,
Which the Patriarch saw.

Hail, Gideon's fleece,
Hail, blossoming rod,
Samson's sweet honeycomb,
Portal of God.

Well fitting it was
That a Son so divine
Should preserve from all touch
Of original sin:

90

Nor suffer by smallest
Defect to be stained,
That Mother whom he
For himself had ordained. Amen.

I dwell in the highest,
and my throne is on the pillar of the clouds.

O Lady, hear my prayer,
and let my cry come unto you.

Let us bless the Lord.
Thanks be to God.

May the souls of the faithful departed,
through the mercy of God, rest in peace. Amen.

At Noon (Sext)

O Lady, make speed to befriend me,
from the hands of the enemy mightily defend me.
Glory be…Alleluia.

HYMN

HAIL, virginal Mother,
Hail, purity's cell,
Fair shrine where the Trinity
Loveth to dwell.

Hail, garden of pleasure,
Celestial balm,
Cedar of chastity,
Martyrdom's palm;

Thou land set apart
From uses profane,
And free from the curse
Which in Adam began;

O city of God,
Thou gate of the east,
In you is all grace,
O joy of the blest. Amen.

As the lily among the thorns,
so is my beloved among the daughters of Adam.

O Lady, hear my prayer,
and let my cry come unto you.

Let us bless the Lord.
Thanks be to God.

May the souls of the faithful departed,
through the mercy of God, rest in peace. Amen.

In the Afternoon (None)
O Lady, make speed to befriend me,
from the hands of the enemy mightily defend me.
Glory be…Alleluia.

HYMN

HAIL, city of refuge,
Hail, David's high tower,
With battlements crowned,
And girded with power;

Filled at your conception
With love and with light,
The dragon by you
Was shorn of his might.

O woman most valiant,
O Judith thrice blest,
As David was nursed
At fair Abisag's breast,

As the saviour of Egypt
Upon Rachel's knee,
So the world's great Redeemer
Was cherished by thee. Amen.

You are all fair, my beloved,
and the original stain was never in you.

O Lady, hear my prayer,
and let my cry come unto you.

Let us bless the Lord.
Thanks be to God.

May the souls of the faithful departed,
through the mercy of God, rest in peace. Amen.

In the Evening (Vespers)
O Lady, make speed to befriend me,
from the hands of the enemy mightily defend me.
Glory be…Alleluia.

MAIDEN AND MOTHER

HYMN

> HAIL, dial of Achas,
> On you the true sun
> Told backward the course
> Which from old he had run;
>
> And, that man might be raised,
> Submitting to shame,
> A little more low
> Than the angels became
>
> You, wrapt in the blaze
> Of his infinite light,
> Dost shine as the morn
> On the confines of night.
>
> As the moon on the lost
> Through obscurity dawns,
> The serpent's destroyer,
> A lily 'mid thorns. Amen.

I made an unfailing light to arise in heaven,
and, as a mist, I overspread the whole earth.

O Lady, hear my prayer,
and let my cry come unto you.

Let us bless the Lord.
Thanks be to God.

May the souls of the faithful departed,
through the mercy of God, rest in peace. Amen.

At Night (Compline)

    May Jesus Christ, your Son,
    reconciled by your prayers, O Lady,
    convert our hearts
    and turn away his anger from us.

    O Lady, make speed to befriend me,
    from the hands of the enemy mightily defend me.
    Glory be…Alleluia.

HYMN

        HAIL, Mother most pure,
        Hail, Virgin renowned,
        Hail, Queen with the stars
        As a diadem crowned;

        Above all the angels,
        In glory untold,
        Standing next to the King
        In a vesture of gold;

        O Mother of mercy,
        O star of the wave,
        O hope of the guilty,
        O light of the grave;

        Through you may we come
        To the haven of rest,
        And see heaven's King
        In the courts of the blest. Amen.

Your name, O Mary, is as oil poured out,
your servants have loved you exceedingly.

O Lady, hear my prayer,
and let my cry come unto you.

Let us bless the Lord.
Thanks be to God.

May the souls of the faithful departed,
through the mercy of God, rest in peace. Amen.

THE COMMENDATION

These praises and prayers
I lay at your feet.
O Virgin of virgins,
O Mary, most sweet.

Be you my true guide
Through this pilgrimage here,
And stand by my side
When death draweth near.
Amen.

Let us pray:
HEAVENLY Father, you prepared a worthy dwelling place
for your divine Son in the womb of the Virgin Mary, pre-
serving her from every stain by the foreseen merits of that
same Son, Jesus Christ, our Redeemer; through Mary's
intercession, free us from sin, cleanse us from all guilt
and bid us come to you so that we may live forever in
peace with you, Father. Amen.

May the blessed Virgin Mary's immaculate conception
be for us an inspiration and a source of confidence in
God's providence. Amen.

OTHER HYMNS FOR MAY:

Daily, Daily, sing to Mary – Ascribed to Bernard of Cluny (twelfth century) Trans. H. Bittleston (1818-86)

Laudes Mariae   87.87.   H. F. Hemy (1818-88)

DAILY, daily, sing to Mary,
Sing, my soul, her praises due;
All her feasts, her actions worship,
With her heart's devotion true.
Lost in wond'ring contemplation
Be her majesty confessed:
Call her Mother, call her Virgin,
Happy Mother, Virgin blest.

She is mighty to deliver;
Call her, trust her lovingly:
When the tempest rages round thee,
She will calm the troubled sea.
Gifts of heaven she has given,
Noble Lady! to our race:
She, the Queen, who decks her subjects
With the light of God's own grace.

Sing, my tongue, the Virgin's trophies,
Who for us her Maker bore;
For the curse of old inflicted,
Peace and blessings to restore.
Sing in songs of praise unending,
Sing the world's majestic Queen;
Weary not nor faint in telling
All the gifts she gives to men.

All my senses, heart, affections,
Strive to sound her glory forth:
Spread abroad, the sweet memorials,
Of the Virgin's priceless worth.
Where the voice of music thrilling,
Where the tongues of eloquence,
That can utter hymns beseeming
All her matchless excellence?

All our joys do flow from Mary,
All then join her praise to sing:
Trembling sing the Virgin Mother,
Mother of our Lord and King.
While we sing her awful glory,
Far above our fancy's reach,
Let our hearts be quick to offer
Love the heart alone can teach.

Queen of the May (Traditional)

BRING flowers of the rarest,
Bring blossoms the fairest,
From garden and woodland and hillside and dale;
Our full hearts are swelling,
Our glad voices telling
The praise of the loveliest flower of the vale.
O Mary, we crown thee with blossoms today,
Queen of the Angels and Queen of the May.
(Repeat)

Their lady they name thee,
Their mistress proclaim thee.
Oh, grant that thy children on earth be as true;
As long as the bowers
Are radiant with flowers,
As long as the azure shall keep its bright hue.
O Mary, we crown thee...

Sing gaily in chorus,
The bright angels o'er us
Re-echo the strains we begin upon earth;
Their harps are repeating
The notes of our greeting,
For Mary herself is the cause of our mirth.
O Mary, we crown thee...

Our voices ascending,
In harmony blending,
Oh, thus may our hearts turn, dear Mother, to thee,
And thus may we prove thee
How truly we love thee,
How dark without Mary life's journey would be.
O Mary, we crown thee...

I'll sing a Hymn to Mary – John Wyse (1825-98)

Crüger   76.76.   D .J. Crüger (1598-1662)

I'LL sing a hymn to Mary,
  The Mother of my God,
The Virgin of all virgins,
  Of David's royal blood.
O teach me, holy Mary,
  A loving song to frame,
When wicked men blaspheme thee,
  To love and bless thy name.

O noble Tower of David,
    Of gold and ivory,
The Ark of God's own promise,
    The gate of heav'n to me,
To live and not to love thee
    Would fill my soul with shame;
When wicked men blaspheme thee,
    I'll love and bless thy name.

The saints are high in glory
    With golden crowns so bright;
But brighter far is Mary
    Upon her throne of light.
O that which God did give thee,
    Let mortal ne'er disclaim;
When wicked men blaspheme thee,
    I'll love and bless thy name.

But in the crown of Mary
    There lies a wondrous gem,
As Queen of all the angels,
    Which Mary shares with them.
"No sin hath e'er defiled thee,"
    So doth our faith proclaim;
When wicked men blaspheme thee,
    I'll love and bless thy name.

This is the Image of the Queen – E. Caswall (1814-78)

Iver   86.86.87.886   H. F. Hemy (1818-88)

THIS is the image of the Queen
Who reigns in bliss above;
Of her who is the hope of men,
Whom men and angels love.
Most holy Mary, at thy feet

PENTECOST

I bend a suppliant knee;
In this thy own sweet month of May,
Dear Mother of my God, I pray,
Do thou remember me.

The homage offered at the feet
Of Mary's image here
To Mary's self at once ascends
Above the starry sphere.
Most holy Mary, at thy feet
I bend a suppliant knee;
In all my joy, in all my pain,
O Virgin born without a stain,
Do thou remember me.

Sweet are the flow'rets we have culled,
This image to adorn;
But sweeter far is Mary's self,
That rose without a thorn.
Most holy Mary, at thy feet
I bend a suppliant knee;
When on the bed of death I lie,
By him who did for sinners die,
Do thou remember me.

O Lady, by the stars that make
A glory round thy head;
And by the pure uplifted hands
That for thy children plead;
When at the Judgement-seat I stand,
And my dread Saviour see;
When waves of night around me roll
And hell is raging for my soul;
O then remember me.

POEM: THE MAY MAGNIFICAT

May is Mary's month, and I
Muse at that and wonder why:
    Her feasts follow reason,
    Dated due to season—

Candlemas, Lady Day;
But the Lady Month, May,
    Why fasten that upon her,
    With a feasting in her honour?

Is it only its being brighter
Than the most are must delight her?
    Is it opportunest
    And flowers finds soonest?

Ask of her, the mighty mother:
Her reply puts this other
    Question: What is Spring?—
    Growth in every thing—

Flesh and fleece, fur and feather,
Grass and greenworld all together;
    Star-eyed strawberry-breasted
    Throstle above her nested

Cluster of bugle blue eggs thin
Forms and warms the life within;
    And bird and blossom swell
    In sod or sheath or shell.

All things rising, all things sizing
Mary sees, sympathising
    With that world of good,
    Nature's motherhood.

104

PENTECOST

Their magnifying of each its kind
With delight calls to mind
    How she did in her stored
    Magnify the Lord.

Well but there was more than this:
Spring's universal bliss
    Much, had much to say
    To offering Mary May.

When drop-of-blood-and-foam-dapple
Bloom lights the orchard-apple
    And thicket and thorp are merry
    With silver-surfèd cherry

And azuring-over greybell makes
Wood banks and brakes wash wet like lakes
    And magic cuckoocall
    Caps, clears, and clinches all—
This ecstasy all through mothering earth
Tells Mary her mirth till Christ's birth
    To remember and exultation
    In God who was her salvation.

Gerard Manley Hopkins, S.J. (1844-89)

31 May
The Visitation of the Blessed Virgin Mary

Today's feast recalls the visit made by Mary to her cousin Elizabeth after the angel had told her that Elizabeth, who had been considered barren for many years, was also to have a child, "for nothing will be impossible with God" (Luke 1:37). Elizabeth's child was to be John the Baptist, the prophet who heralded Our Lord's coming (see Luke 3:1-22). Filled with the Holy Spirit, Elizabeth greets Mary in the words that have become the second sentence of the "Hail Mary," to which Mary responds with her song of praise drawn from the Psalms and other scriptural sources, the Magnificat *(see Luke 1:39-48).*

The celebration of this feast originated with the Franciscans, when St Bonaventure requested its introduction at the General Chapter of 1236. Pope Pius V finally made it universal, with the date of 2 July. This date was changed to the present one in the general revision to the Calendar of 1969, to stress its scriptural links with the Annunciation (25 March) and the Birthday of St John the Baptist (24 June) by placing it between them. Mary's song of praise and thanksgiving, the Magnificat, *is both her personal response to Elizabeth's greeting and a universal expression of thanks for the gift of the Incarnation. This is why it is sung every day at vespers, so the Visitation is commemorated on every day of the year, not just today.*

The beautiful words of the Magnificat *have inspired many great composers to set it to music. It can be heard in Roman Catholic, Anglican, Russian Orthodox, and Greek Orthodox churches.*

(Adapted from Butler's Lives of the Saints, *May volume*

MAGNIFICAT

Vatican Plainsong

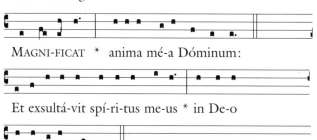

MAGNI-FICAT * anima mé-a Dóminum:

Et exsultá-vit spí-ri-tus me-us * in De-o

sa-lu-tá-ri me-o:

Quia respexit humilitatem ancillae suae: * ecce enim ex hoc beatam me dicent omnes generationes.

Quia fecit mihi magna qui potens est: * et sanctum nomen ejus.

Et misericordia ejus a progenie in progenies * timentibus eum.

Fecit potentiam in brachio suo: * dispersit superbos mente cordis sui.

Deposuit potentes de sede, * et exaltavit humiles.

Esurientes implevit bonis: * et divites dimisit inanes.

Suscepit Israel, puerum suum, * recordatus misericordiae suae.

Sicut locutus est ad patres nostros, * Abraham, et semini ejus in saecula.

Gloria Patri, et Filio, * et Spiritu Sancto.

Sicut erat in principio, et nunc, et semper, * et in saecula saeculorum. Amen.

My soul doth magnify the Lord: and my spirit hath rejoiced in God my Saviour.

For he hath regarded: the lowliness of his handmaiden.

For behold from henceforth: all generations shall call me blessed.

For he that is mighty hath magnified me: and holy is his Name.

And his mercy is on them that fear him: throughout all generations.

He hath shewed strength with his arm: he hath scattered the proud in the imagination of their hearts.

He hath put down the mighty from their seat: and hath exalted the humble and meek.

He hath filled the hungry with good things: and the rich he hath sent empty away.

He remembering his mercy hath holpen his servant Israel: as he promised to our forefathers, Abraham and his seed forever.

(King James Bible)

Glory be to the Father, and to the Son, and to the Holy Spirit; as it was in the beginning, is now, and ever shall be: world without end. Amen.

Music: to the Latin text, Tomás Luís de Victoria, Magnificat primi toni (1600); to the English King James version, Charles Villiers Stanford, Magnificat in G., Opus 81 (1904); Magnificat in A, Opus 12 (1880).

The Greek Orthodox add the Troparion *(Refrain), "Greater in honour than the cherubim, and glorious incomparably more than the seraphim; thou who inviolate didst bring forth God the Word, and art indeed the Mother of God: thee do we magnify" after each verse. There is a musical setting to this form by John Tavener, written for the choir of King's College, Cambridge, in 1986.*

GOSPEL READING

In those days Mary arose and went with haste into the hill country, to a city of Judah, and she entered the house of Zechariah and greeted Elizabeth. And when Elizabeth hear the greeting of Mary, the babe leaped in her womb; and Elizabeth was filled with the Holy Spirit and she exclaimed with a loud cry, "Blessed are you among women, and blessed is the fruit of your womb! And why is this granted to me, that the mother of my Lord should come to me? For behold, when the voice of your greeting came to my ears, the babe in my womb leaped for joy. And blessed is she who believed that there would be a fulfilment of what was spoken to her from the Lord."

And Mary said,

"My soul magnifies the Lord,
and my spirit rejoices in God my Saviour,
for he has regarded the low estate of his handmaiden.
For behold, henceforth all generations will call me
blessed;
for he who is mighty has done great things for me,
and holy is his name.
And his mercy is on those who fear him
from generation to generation.
He has shown strength with his arm,
he has scattered the proud in the imagination of
their hearts,
he has put down the mighty from their thrones,
and exalted those of low degree;
he has filled the hungry with good things,
and the rich he has sent empty away.
He has helped his servant Israel,
in remembrance of his mercy,

as he spoke to our fathers,
to Abraham and to his posterity for ever."
And Mary remained with her about three months, and
returned to her home.

Luke 1:39-56

COLLECT

FAMULIS tuis, quaesumus, Domine, caelestis gratiae
munus impertire: ut, quibus beatae Virginis partus exsti-
tit salutis exordium; Visitationis ejus votiva solemnitas
pacis tribuat incrementum.

*Bestow the gift of divine grace on your servants, Lord. The
Blessed Virgin's childbearing was the beginning of salvation:
may this festival of her visiting bring us an increase of peace.*

ALLELUIA

Alleluia, alleluia.
Felix es, sacra Virgo Maria, et omni laude dignissima:
quia ex te ortus est sol justitiae Christus Deus noster.
Alleluia.

Alleluia, alleluia.
Holy Virgin Mary, happy and most worthy of all praise; the
Sun of Justice, Jesus Christ our God,
has taken from you his rising.
Alleluia.

BREVIARY READING:

Not only blessed among women, but with an eminent
blessing among all blessed women. Nor is the fruit of her
womb blessed after the manner of the saints, but as the
Apostle says, "Of whom is Christ according to the flesh,
who is over all things, God blessed for ever." And again:

110

"Our earth gave its fruit when the same Virgin, whose body was of our earth, gave birth to a Son co-equal to his Father in his divinity, though consubstantial with his Mother in the truth of his humanity."

From a homily by The Venerable Bede (673-735)

A LEGEND: *As Mary went through the Thorn Forest*

As Mary was returning from her visit to Elizabeth, bearing Jesus beneath her heart, she had to pass through a forest of thorns that for seven long years had borne no leaves. For a moment she hesitated to go on in the fading twilight. But then she thought of the Son of the Almighty in her womb and of Joseph, who was waiting for her. So she stepped forward into the dark thicket— which was suddenly bathed in golden light, and as she bore the Babe through the forest, so the thorns brought forth roses.

BOGORÓDITSE DYÉVO — *A Russian "Hail Mary"*

Bogoródise Dyévo, ráduyssya,
Blagodatnaya Maríye,
Gosspód ss Tobóyu;
blagosslovyéna Ty v zhenákhi blagosslovyén
plod chryéva Tvoyevo,
yáko Sspássa rodilá yeessí dush náshikh.

Set to music by Avro Pärt (b. 1935)

Virgin Lady, rejoice;
Gracious Mary,
The Lord is with you.
Blessed are you among women,
and blessed is the fruit of your womb,
You who bore the one who would save our souls.

Translated by Christine Grainger

111

The Immaculate Heart of Mary

Particular devotion to the Heart of Mary can be traced to the thirteenth and fourteenth centuries, but it began to emerge more strongly in the sixteenth century, and its cult was then developed above all by St John Eudes (1601-80) in the seventeenth. He composed a Mass and Office for the Heart of Mary, which was first performed in the cathedral of Autun in 1648. He also wrote the treatise The Admirable Heart of the Mother of God, *which was not published until after his death. Permission to celebrate the feast was granted first to several religious Orders and then in 1805 to any diocese that asked. The devotion spread throughout the nineteenth century, and the form of Office and Mass for the feast was formally approved in 1855, the year after the dogmatic declaration of the Immaculate Conception. On 8 December 1942, Pope Pius XII solemnly consecrated the universe to the Heart of Mary, and it was made a world-wide feast, celebrated on 22 August (now the Queenship of Mary) in 1944. The 1969 Calendar reform made it an optional memorial and moved it to the present date.*

HYMN

> AD te clamamus, audi nos,
> Virgo, regina saeculi;
> Et in nocte custodi nos
> Sicut pupillam oculi.

> *O Maiden, Queen of all the earth,*
> *Receive the vows our hearts pour forth;*
> *And as the apple of an eye*
> *To keep us in this night be nigh.*

PENTECOST

Iam tibi, mater, septies
In die laudem diximus,
Sit nobis in te requies
Sub umbra cuius vivimus.

Blest Mother, unto thee we pray,
And laud thee seven times a day;
Thy rest unto thy people give,
Beneath whose guardian wing we live.

Fessos diurnis aestibus
Nos somno pacis refove,
Nobisque quiescentibus
Tu fraudes hostis remove.

Grant us from toils of day release
In the refreshing sleep of peace;
And as this night we lie at rest,
Let not the foe disturb our breast.

Stella fulgore praedita,
Lux iucunda, lux celebris,
In tuas laudes excita
Nos mane pulsis tenebris.

O Star elect that shinest bright
In most serene and gladsome light,
With day's new dawn thy servants raise
Unharmed by night to chant thy praise.

An evening hymn to Our Lady from a fifteenth-century French breviary.
The "seven times a day" refers to the traditional seven "hours" of the Office.

FROM THE MASS: ENTRANCE ANTIPHON

My heart rejoices in your saving power. I will sing to the Lord for his goodness to me. *(Ps.12:6)*

OPENING PRAYER

FATHER, you prepared the heart of the Virgin Mary to be a fitting home for your Holy Spirit. By her prayers may we become a more worthy temple of your glory. Grant this through our Lord Jesus Christ, your Son, who lives and reigns with you and the Holy Spirit, one God for ever and ever.

PRAYER OVER THE GIFTS

LORD, accept the prayers and gifts we offer in honour of Mary, the Mother of God. May they please you and bring us your help and forgiveness. We ask this in the name of Jesus the Lord.

COMMUNION ANTIPHON

Mary treasured all these words and pondered them in her heart. *(Luke 2:19)*

PRAYER AFTER COMMUNION

LORD, you have given us the sacrament of eternal redemption. May we who honour the Mother of your Son rejoice in the abundance of your blessings and experience the deepening of your life within us. We ask this through Christ our Lord.

PRAYER OF CONSECRATION
TO THE IMMACULATE HEART OF MARY

O Immaculate Heart of Mary, ardent with goodness, show your love towards us. May the flame of your heart, O Mary, descend on all mankind.

ANTHEM: SALVE REGINA

Sung at compline from the Saturday before Trinity Sunday until Advent.

Composed at the end of the eleventh century and adopted above all by the Cistercians, originally as a processional hymn to be sung on saints' days. The Benedictines were instructed to sing it after compline, which lay people often attended, and the tunefulness of its plainchant setting made it extremely popular. It became part of the service of Benediction, especially on Saturdays. For the music, see under Advent, p. 11.

SALVE Regina, mater misericordiae:
vita, dulcedo, et spes nostra, salve.
Ad te clamamus, exules filii Hevae.
Ad te suspiramus, gementes et flentes,
in hac lacrymarum valle.
Eia ergo, advocata nostra,
illos tuos misericordes oculos
ad nos converte.
Et JESUM, benedictum fructum ventris tui,
nobis post hoc exilium ostende.
O clemens, O pia, O dulcis Virgo Maria.

℣. Ora pro nobis, sancta Dei Genitrix.
℞. Ut digni efficiamur promissionibus Christi.

Oremus:

OMNIPOTENS, sempiterne Deus, qui gloriosae Virginis Matris Mariae corpus et animam, ut dignum Filii tui habitaculum effici mereretur, Spiritu Sancto cooperante, praeparisti; da, ut cujus commemoratione laetemur, ejus pia intercessione ab instantibus malis et a morte perpetua liberemur. Per eundem Christum Dominum nostrum. Amen.

Hail, holy Queen, Mother of mercy;
Hail, our life, our sweetness and our hope!
To thee do we cry, poor banished children of Eve,
to thee do we send up our sighs,
mourning and weeping in this vale of tears.
Turn then, most gracious Advocate,
thine eyes of mercy towards us; and after this, our exile
show unto us the blessed fruit of thy womb, Jesus.
O clement, O loving, O sweet Virgin Mary!

℣. *Pray for us, holy Mother of God,*
℟. *That we may be worthy of the promises of Christ.*

Let us pray:
Almighty, eternal God, who with the help of the Holy Spirit
have prepared the body and soul of the glorious Virgin Mary
to be the worthy home of your Son, grant that we who rejoice
in her memory may, by her holy prayers, be freed from all pre-
sent evils and from everlasting death. Through the same
Christ our Lord. Amen.

Trans. Denis Hayes

HYMN: AVE MARIS STELLA *Vatican Plainsong*

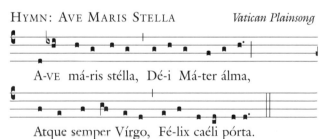

A-ve má-ris stélla, Dé-i Má-ter álma,

Atque semper Vírgo, Fé-lix caéli pórta.

Sumens illud Ave
Gabrielis ore,
Funda nos in pace,
Mutans Hevae nomen.

116

Solve vincla reis,
Profer lumen caecis,
Mala nostra pelle,
Bona cuncta posce.

Monstra te esse Matrem,
Sumat per te preces,
Qui pro nobis natus,
Tulit esse tuus.

Virgo singularis,
Inter omnes mitis,
Nos culpis solutos,
Mites fac et castos.

Vitam praesta puram,
Iter para tutum,
Ut videntes Jesum,
Semper collaetemur.

Sit laus Deo Patri,
Summo Christo decus,
Spiritui Sancto,
Tribus honor unus.

Formerly attributed to St Bernard, but known in a ninth-century manuscript. The most likely author is Paul the Deacon (c. 720-800), a monk of Monte Cassino. For the more familiar musical setting and other translations, see under Autumn, pp. 186-90. There is a musical setting by Sir Edward Elgar, his Opus 2/3 (1887).

> *Star of ocean, lead us;*
> *God for Mother claims thee,*
> *Ever-Virgin names thee;*
> *Gate of heaven, speed us,*

MAIDEN AND MOTHER

AVE to thee crying,
Gabriel went before us;
Peace do thou restore us,
EVA's knot untying.

Loose the bonds that chain us,
Darkened eyes enlighten,
Clouded prospects brighten,
Heavenly mercies gain us.

For thy sons thou carest;
Offer Christ our praying—
Still thy word obeying—
Whom on earth thou barest.

Purer, kinder maiden
God did never fashion;
Pureness and compassion
Grant to hearts sin-laden.

From that sin release us,
Shield us, heavenward faring—
Heaven, that is but sharing
In thy joy with Jesus.

Honour, praise and merit
To our God address we;
Three in One confess we,
Father, Son, and Spirit.

Trans. R. A. Knox (1888-1957)

HYMN: MAIDEN, YET A MOTHER

Ronald A. Knox (1888-1957), based on verses from Canto 33 of the Paradiso by Dante Alighieri (1265-1321)

Une Vraie Crainte   65.65.ds   *French carol*

MAIDEN, yet a Mother,
Daughter of thy Son,
High beyond all other—
Lowlier is none;
Thou the consummation
Planned by God's decree,
When our lost creation
Nobler rose in thee!

119

Thus his place preparèd,
He who all things made
'Mid his creatures tarried,
In thy bosom laid;
There his love he nourished—
Warmth that gave increase
To the Root whence flourished
Our eternal peace.

Noon on Sion's mountain
Is thy charity;
Hope its living fountain
Finds, on earth, in thee:
Lady, such thy power,
He, who grace would buy
Not as of thy dower,
Without wings would fly.

Nor alone thou hearest
When thy name we hail;
Often thou art nearest
When out voices fail;
Mirrored in thy fashion
All creation's good,
Mercy, might, compassion
Grace thy womanhood.

Lady, lest our vision,
Striving heavenward, fail,
Still let thy petition
With thy Son prevail,
Unto whom all merit,
Power and majesty,
With the Holy Spirit
And the Father be.

HAIL, QUEEN OF HEAVEN

Stella   88.88.88.   *H. F. Hemy (1818-88)*

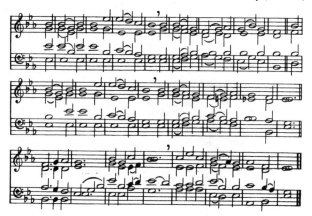

HAIL, Queen of heav'n, the ocean star
Guide of the wand'rer here below;
Thrown on life's surge, we claim thy care;
Save us from peril and from woe.
Mother of Christ, Star of the Sea,
Pray for the wanderer, pray for me.

O gentle, chaste and spotless Maid,
We sinners make our prayers through thee;
Remind thy Son that he has paid
The price of our iniquity.
Virgin most pure, Star of the Sea,
Pray for the sinner, pray for me.

Sojourners in this vale of tears,
To thee, blest advocate, we cry;
Pity our sorrows, calm our fears

121

And soothe with hope our misery.
Refuge in grief, Star of the Sea,
Pray for the mourner, pray for me.

And while to him who reigns above,
In Godhead One, in Persons Three,
The source of life, of grace, of love,
Homage we pay on bended knee,
Do thou, bright Queen, Star of the Sea,
Pray for thy children, pray for me.

John Lingard (1771-1851)

ORDINARY TIME I

SUMMER

Celebrations of Our Lady during this period include
Our Lady of Perpetual Help on 27 June;
Our Lady of Mount Carmel, on 16 July;
The Assumption of the B.V.M., on 15 August;
The Queenship of Mary, on 22 August;
The Birthday of Our Lady, on 8 September;
Our Lady of Sorrows, on 15 September;
and, in England and Wales,
Our Lady of Ransom, on 24 September.

Other commemorations related to her are
The Birthday of St John the Baptist, on 24 June;
SS Joachim and Anne, parents of the B.V.M., on 26 July;
During Ordinary Time, the Saturday Mass of Our Lady
can be celebrated if no solemnity, feast,
or obligatory memorial falls on that particular Saturday.

The liturgical colour for the season is green, but the colour
used for feasts of Our Lady is white, denoting rejoicing.

ST LUKE PAINTING THE VIRGIN AND CHILD
*(based on a sixteenth-century Russian icon of the Pskov
school, in the church of Oposka)*

27 June
Our Lady of Perpetual Help

The title derives from an icon, probably painted in Crete in the fourteenth century, which was brought to Rome in 1499 and acquired a reputation for working wonders. Originally in the church of St Matthew, it was transferred to that of St Alphonsus de' Ligouri in 1869, where the Redemptorists founded a sodality of Our Lady under this title and of St Alphonsus in 1871. This was raised to the rank of an arch-sodality in 1876. The icon is one of several that have been attributed to St Luke, claimed as the first icon-painter from a legend that he painted an icon of the Virgin and Child (see facing page).

The feast was never in the universal Calendar; it was observed in Rome on 26 April, and elsewhere "by special grant" on 27 June. Our Lady of Perpetual Help is the patron saint of Haiti.

PRAYER TO OUR MOTHER OF PERPETUAL HELP

MOTHER of perpetual help, with the greatest confidence we turn to you in prayer, inspired by the example of your life.

We think of you at that moment when, full of faith and trust, you accepted God's call to be the Mother of our Saviour. Help us to accept our own calling in life.

When you learned that Elizabeth was to be a mother also you went to share her joy and to help her. May we have that same deep concern for the needs of others.

We think of you at the foot of the cross, and the sorrow you must have experienced at that time. But great was your joy when your Son rose victorious from the dead, destroying the power of evil.

Mother of sorrows, help us not to lose heart when we experience trials and disappointments in our lives. Help us to follow your example of faith so that we may also share in the joy of the resurrection. Amen.

FROM THE MASS

From the Roman Missal (pre-1973)

COLLECT

LORD Jesus Christ, by whose gift Mary thy Mother, that Mary whose glorious image we revere, is our mother too, and ready at all times to succour us; we pray thee, grant that we, who earnestly beg her maternal help, may be counted worthy to reap through all eternity the fruit of thy redeeming work.

GRADUAL AND ALLELUIA

FAIR and gentle art thou, daughter of Sion; beautiful as the moon, bright as the sun, terrible as an army drawn up for battle. What blessing the power of the Lord has granted thee, making use of thee to bring our enemies to nothing!

Alleluia, alleluia. Hail Mary, full of grace, the Lord is with thee; blessed art thou among women. Alleluia.
(based on Song of Songs 6:3, 9; Judith 13:22; Luke 1:28)

Gospel Reading

Standing by the cross of Jesus were his mother, and his mother's sister, Mary the wife of Clopas, and Mary Magdalen. When Jesus saw his mother, and the disciple whom he loved standing near, he said to his mother, "Woman, behold, your son!" Then he said to the disciple, "Behold, your mother!" And from that hour the disciple took her to his own home.

John 19:25-7

Prayer

Mary,
How many times have I found,
when I come to appeal to you,
that you have healed the aching wounds of my heart.

Guido Gezelle

To Our Lady of Good Counsel

MOST glorious Virgin, chosen by the eternal Wisdom to be the Mother of the eternal Word in the flesh, thou who art the treasurer of God's graces and the advocate of sinners, I thy most unworthy servant turn to thee; be pleased to guide and counsel me in this vale of tears. Obtain for me, through the precious Blood of thy divine Son, the forgiveness of my sins, the salvation of my soul, and the means necessary to bring it about. Obtain also for holy Church victory over her enemies and the spread of the kingdom of Jesus Christ over the whole earth. Amen.

16 July
Our Lady of Mount Carmel

Devotion to Our Lady under this title has been spread by the Brothers of the Blessed Virgin Mary of Mount Carmel, or Carmelites, who take their name from the mountain near Haifa in the Holy Land where the prophet Elijah dwelt in a cave. Nearby on the main road to Nazareth is Mary's Well, traditionally the place where the archangel Gabriel appeared to Mary. The Carmelites based their life of prayer on Elijah and saw Mary's life of total obedience to the will of God as symbolizing their vows. They were driven from Mount Carmel by the Saracens in 1242 and settled in various places in Europe, guided, it is said, by Our Lady. Because of this guidance, they developed a special devotion to Mary as Star of the Sea. In England, their Carmel at Aylesford in Kent remains a popular place of pilgrimage to this day. It is venerated as the place where, in 1251, Our Lady gave St Simon Stock, the English prior general, the brown garment and scapular which the Carmelites still wear. This scapular is also worn by lay members of the Confraternity of Our Lady of Mount Carmel, with the assurance given by the apparition that those who wear it will be saved.

Our Lady of Mount Carmel is patron of Chile, proclaimed by Bernardo O'Higgins, who promised her this title if he defeated the Spanish colonizers, which he did decisively at Maipú in 1818, afterwards building a shrine there in her honour.

PRAYER IN SPECIAL NEED

To Our Lady of Mount Carmel

O MOST beautiful flower of Mount Carmel,
Fruitful Vine, Splendour of Heaven,
Blessed Mother of the Son of God, Immaculate Virgin,
assist me in this my necessity.
O Star of the Sea, help me and show me
herein you are my Mother.

O Holy Mary, Mother of God,
Queen of Heaven and Earth,
I humbly beseech you from the bottom of my heart
to succour me in this necessity;
there are none that can withstand your power.

O, show me herein you are my Mother;
O Mary, conceived without sin,
Pray for us who have recourse to thee.
(Three times)

Sweet Mother,
I place this cause in your hands.
(Three times)

FROM THE MASS
FOR OUR LADY OF MOUNT CARMEL

From the Layman's Missal and Prayer Book (1962)

ENTRANCE ANTIPHON

REJOICE we all in the Lord, as we keep holiday in Mary's
honour; that blessed maiden whose feast makes angels

rejoice and sets them praising the Son of God. Joyful the thoughts that well up from my heart, a King's honour for thy theme.

COLLECT

GOD, who hast honoured the Order of Carmel by giving the most blessed Mother Mary, ever-virgin, that special title, grant to us this grace, that we who are today commemorating her with solemn observance may be counted worthy, under the shield of her protection, to attain everlasting happiness.

GRADUAL

BENEDICTA et venerabilis es, Virgo Maria: quae sine tactu pudoris inventa es mater Salvatoris. Virgo Dei Genitrix, quem totus non capit orbis, in tua se clausit viscera factus homo.

Mary, Virgin, you are blessed and worthy of our homage; for with maidenhood unsullied you became the Saviour's Mother. God's Virgin Mother! The whole wide world cannot contain him, yet he became a man and shut himself within your womb.

ALLELUIA

Alleluia, alleuia.
Per te, Dei Genitrix, nobis est vita perdita data: quae de caelo suscepisti prolem, et mundo genuisti Salvatorem.
Alleluia.

Alleluia, alleluia.
Through you, God's Mother, the life that was lost has been restored to us. You took your child from heaven, and gave him to the world to be its Saviour.
Alleluia!

HYMN TO THE MOTHER OF GOD

WHERE shall I make my beginning to mourn
The deeds of my wretched life?
What first fruits shall I lay down, O Christ,
To this my present weeping?
But as thou art merciful,
Grant me forgiveness of sin.
Eleison me, O Theos, eleison me.

Come wretched soul, with thy flesh,
Confess to the Maker of all;
And from now leave thy past folly
And bring tears of repentance to God.
Pomilui mia, Boge, pomilui mia.
I rivalled in transgression Adam first created,
And I knew myself naked of God,
Of the everlasting kingdom, and of the delight,
because of my sins.
Have mercy upon me, O God, have mercy upon me.

Alas unto me, wretched soul.
How like thou art to the first Eve!
Evil thou saw, and were grievously wounded,
And the tree thou touched,
And recklessly tasted the food of folly.
Eleison me, O Theos, eleison me.
Instead of Eve of the flesh, I have Eve of the mind,
In thoughts of sensual passion, seemingly sweet,
But ever tasting of the bitter down-gulping.
Pomilui mia, Boge, pomilui mia.

Adam was justly banished from Eden, O Saviour,
For not keeping one commandment of thine;

131

MAIDEN AND MOTHER

What then shall I suffer,
Ever thrusting aside thy words of life?

To you, O Woman full of grace,
The angelic choirs and the human race,
All creation rejoices.
O sanctified Temple, mystical Paradise,
And glory of virgins.
In you, O Woman full of grace,
All creation rejoices.
All praise be to you.

Text from the Liturgy of St Basil, used in the Greek and Russian Orthodox Churches. The English version given here is used in a musical setting by John Tavener (b. 1944), 1985.

TOTUS TUUS

Totus tuus sum, Maria,
Mater nostri Redemptoris,
Virgo Dei, virgo pia,
Mater mundi Salvatoris,
Totus tuus sum, Maria.

I am all yours, Mary,
Mother of our Redeemer,
Virgin of God, holy virgin,
Mother of the Saviour of the world,
I am all yours, Mary.

Maria Boguslawska. There is a musical setting by Henryk Górecki (b. 1933).

15 August
The Assumption of
the Blessed Virgin Mary into Heaven

THIS is the most significant and most popular feast in the Marian calendar because it commemorates the day of her death. The belief that Mary was taken up body and soul into heaven is an ancient one, being connected by the fourth or fifth century to stories of the apostles finding her tomb empty after her death. The feast spread from the East to Rome in the seventh century, but under the name of the Dormition ("falling asleep"), as it is still known in the East, until the 770s, when it took the title of the Assumption in the Gregorian Sacramentary. The essence of the belief is that "the sinless body which bore the Incarnate Word could not suffer the decay that follows death. Mary was with her Son in his sufferings and she is with him in his triumph; she already has that fullness of glory that we hope to have at the end of time" (Layman's Missal). *In the Middle Ages Peter Abelard argued that since Christ had the power to save his mother from the corruption of the tomb, it was fitting that he should do so. Belief in the doctrine spread widely, but it was not until 1950 that Pope Pius XII declared it an article of faith, in his Bull* Munificentissimus Deus.

A GREAT portent appeared in heaven; a woman with the sun her mantle, the moon her footstool, and twelve stars set as a crown about her head. Sing to the Lord a song that is new; for wonderful are the deeds he has wrought.
Rev. 12:1; Ps. 97:1, Entrance Chant from the Mass

Hail, O Queen of heaven enthroned!
Hail, by angels Mistress owned!
From the prayer Ave, Regina caelorum

133

From eternity in the beginning he created me and for eternity I shall remain. I ministered before him in the holy temple and thus I was established in Jerusalem.

Eccl. 24:9-10.

PRAYERS AND CHANTS FROM THE MASS
From the Layman's Missal and Prayer Book (1962)

ENTRANCE ANTIPHON

And now, in heaven, a great portent appeared; a woman that wore the sun for her mantle, with the moon under her feet, and a crown of twelve stars about her head.

Rev. 12:1

OPENING PRAYER

ALMIGHTY and everliving God, you have taken up the sinless Virgin Mary, the Mother of your Son, body and soul into the glory of heaven. May our minds be always fixed on things above, that we too may be able to have part in that glory.

RESPONSORIAL PSALM AND ALLELUIA

Daughters of kings are among your ladies of honour;
at your right hand stands the queen in gold of Ophir.
Hear, O daughter, consider and incline your ear;
forget your people and your father's house....
At your right hand stands the queen in gold of Ophir.
And the king will desire your beauty.
Since he is your lord, bow to him....
In many-coloured robes she is led to the king;
behind her the virgins, her companions, follow.
With joy and gladness they are led along
as they enter the palace of the king.
At your right hand stands the queen in gold of Ophir.

Psalm 45 (44):9, 10, 11, 12, 14-15

SUMMER

Alleluia, alleluia!
Mary has been taken up into heaven;
choirs of angels, rejoice.
Alleluia.

FROM THE PREFACE

TODAY the Virgin Mother of God
was taken up into heaven to be the beginning and the
pattern of the Church in its perfection, and a sign of
hope and comfort for your people on their pilgrim way.
You would not allow decay to touch her body, for she
had given birth to your Son, the Lord of all life,
in the glory of the incarnation.

COMMUNION ANTIPHON

Every generation will call me blessed, for great indeed are
the things the Almighty has done for me.

Luke 2:48-9

POSTCOMMUNION

LORD, we pray that we may be brought to a glorious resurrection, through the merits and prayers of the blessed
Virgin Mary, who was taken up into heaven.

HYMN

For the Dormition of the Mother of God

O ye apostles,
assembled here from the ends of the earth,
bury my body in Gethsemane;
and Thou my Son and God, receive my spirit.

*From the liturgy of St Basil. In addition to the musical setting by
John Tavener (b.1944), there is one by Charles-Marie Widor (1844-1937).*

135

AVE MARIA

AVE Maria, Mater Dei, regina,
    Caeli domina, mundi imperatrix inferni.
Miserere mei et totius populi christiani;
    Et ne permittas nos mortaliter peccare,
Sed tuam sanctissimam voluntatem adimplere.
    Amen.

William Cornysh (d. 1523)

Hail, Mary, Mother of God and queen,
    Lady of heaven and empress of the world below.
Have mercy on me and on all Christian people;
    And let us not fall into mortal sin,
But let us perfectly fulfil your most holy will.
    Amen.

Trans. Denis Hayes

MOTETTE

TU virginum corona,
tu nobis pacem dona,
tu nobis pacem dona,
tu consolare affectus,
unde suspirat cor. *(Repeat from line 1)*
Unde, unde suspirat,
suspirat cor,
unde suspirat cor.
(Two-bar music interlude)
Tu virginum corona,
tu nobis pacem dona,
tu nobis pacem dona,
tu consolare affectus,
unde suspirat cor,
unde suspirat cor.

136

Tu virginum corona,
tu nobis pacem dona,
tu nobis pacem dona,
tu consolare affectus,
unde suspirat cor,
unde, unde suspirat,
suspirat cor,
tu consolare affectus,
unde suspirat cor,
unde, unde suspirat cor,
unde suspirat cor.

Arranged with repeats as in Exultate, jubilate (KV165 [158a])
by Wolfgang Amadeus Mozart (1756-91)

Crown of Virgins,
grant us peace,
grant us peace,
to give consolation
for which the heart longs. *(Repeat from line 1)*
Whence, whence longs,
the heart longs,
whence the heart sighs,
(Two-bar music interlude)
Crown of Virgins,
grant us peace,
grant us peace,
to give consolation,
for which the heart longs,
whence the heart sighs.

Crown of Virgins,
grant us peace,
grant us peace,
to give consolation,
for which the heart longs,
whence, whence longs, sighs the heart,
to give consolation,
for which the heart longs,
whence, whence the heart longs,
whence the heart sighs.

Trans. Denis Hayes

MOTET: *Assumpta est Maria*

Assumpta est Maria in caelum.
Gaudent angeli laudantes; benedicunt Dominum.

Into heaven is Mary received;
The angels with praises rejoice and bless the Lord.

MISSA

Assumpta est Maria in caelum.
Gaudete et exsultate omnes recti corde.
Quia hodie Maria Virgo cum Christo
Regnat in aeternum.
Quae est ista, quae progreditur
Quasi aurora consurgens,
Pulchra ut luna, electa ut sol,
Terribilis ut castrorum acies ordinata?

Gaudete omnes recti corde.
Quia hodie Maria Virgo cum Christo
Regnat in aeternum.

SUMMER

Sicut lilium inter spinas,
Sic amica mea, inter filias Adamae.
Alleluia.

Words from the Book of Revelation and the Song of Songs, arranged for
Motet by Giovanni Pierluisi da Palestrina (c. 1525-94)

MISSA

Into heaven is Mary received;
The angels with praises rejoice and bless the Lord.

Let all rejoice and with righteous heart be glad;
For today the Virgin Mary reigns with Christ
Through all eternity.
Who is she who proceeds
Like the rising dawn, beautiful as the moon,
Clothed like the sun,
Fearful as a castle adorned with weaponry?

Let all rejoice and with righteous heart be glad;
For today the Virgin Mary reigns with Christ
Through all eternity.

Like a lily among thorns,
So is my love among the daughters of Adam.
Alleluia.

NOVENA PRAYER *(Recited after Vespers from 6 to 15 August)*

O GLORIOUS Queen of all the heavenly host, whose sacred body, the immaculate temple of the Divinity, is now assumed into heaven, I unite my voice to the choir of angels who celebrate thy triumph. Winter is now past for thee *(Song of Songs 2:3)*. O fervent follower of thy crucified Son, in this world, like him thou hadst no part in its perishable possessions, but now all the treasures of heaven are thine; they are thine to enjoy, and thine to distribute; for thy intercession is now an infinite treasure to us, which they that use become the friends of God *(Wisd. 7:14)*. Thou wert buried in obscurity in this valley of tears, but now thou art compared with the light and art found before it *(Wisd. 7:29)*.

O Mother of God, elevated to the highest pinnacle of glory, should not thy triumphant exaltation encourage us to despise this world and aspire after the next? For, O amiable Vigin, how short were thy sufferings on earth, yet, for all eternity thou shalt be admired in the holy assembly; among the elect thou shalt have praise, and among the blessed thou shalt be blessed *(Ecclus. 24:3, 4)*.

Look down then with compassion on us, poor banished children of Eve; draw our hearts after thee by filial confidence and vigorous exertions to imitate thy virtues; above all, obtain for us true humility, which neither seeks nor values any earthly distinction, poverty of spirit, purity of heart, that thirst after the strong and living God which can never be satisfied until his glory appears, and such ardent love of our divine Spouse as may cause us to despise the whole world and incessantly sigh after those eternal joys which the eye hath not seen, nor ear heard, neither hath it entered into the heart of man to conceive *(1 Cor. 2:9)*. Amen. *From the Choir Manual of the Little Office of the B.V.M.*

HYMN: *The Assumption*
Assumpta est   75.75.   *A.G.M.*

WHO is she ascends so high,
 Next the heavenly King,
Round about whom angels fly
 And her praises sing?

Who is she adorned with light,
 Makes the sun her robe,
At whose feet the queen of night
 Lays her changing globe?

This is she in whose pure womb
 Heaven's Prince remained;
Therefore in no earthly tomb
 Can she be contained.

Heaven she was, which held that fire,
 Whence the world took light,
And to heaven doth now aspire
 Flames with flames t'unite.

She that did so clearly shine
  When our day begun,
See how bright her beams decline:
  Now she sits with the Sun.

Sir John Beaumont (1583-1627)

HYMN: *The Assumption*

Assumption   L.M.   H. Stanley Taylor

O LADY Mary, thy bright crown
Is no mere crown of majesty;
For with the reflex of his own
Resplendent thorns Christ circled thee.

142

The red rose of this Passion tide
Doth take a deeper hue from thee,
In the five wounds of Jesus dyed,
And in thy bleeding thoughts, Mary.

The soldier struck a triple stroke
That smote thy Jesus on the tree;
He broke the Heart of hearts and broke
The saint's and Mother's hearts in thee.

Thy Son went up the angels' ways,
His passion ended; but, ah me!
Thou found'st the road of further days
A longer way to Calvary.

On the hard cross of hopes deferred
Thou hung'st in living agony,
Until the mortal dreaded word,
Which chills our mirth, spake mirth to thee.

The Angel Death, from this cold tomb
Of life, did roll the stone away,
And he thou barest in the womb
Caught thee at last into the day.

Francis Thompson (1859-1907)

HYMN OF PRAISE
ATTRIBUTED TO ST JOHN OF DAMASCUS

THE angelic host, the race of men, all creation rejoices over thee, Mary, for thou art full of grace, a hallowed temple, a spiritual paradise. From thee, most glorious of virgins, our God took flesh; he who at the beginning of time was already God became thy child. He made thy womb his throne; he, whom the heavens cannot hold, found there his resting-place. All creation rejoices over thee. Glory be thine, Mary, for thou art full of grace.

143

22 August
The Queenship of Mary

Honouring Mary as Queen has always been implied by the title "Our Lady," but there was no separate feast to celebrate her under this title until 1954, when it was established to mark the centenary of the declaration of the dogma of the Immaculate Conception. It was first observed on 31 May but in the Calendar reform of 1969 was moved to 22 August, the "octave day" of (eighth day after) the Assumption, while the Visitation replaced it on 31 May. The Queenship of Mary now ranks as an obligatory memorial.

ANTIPHON

Now a great sign appeared in heaven, a woman adorned with the sun, standing on the moon, with twelve stars on her head for a crown. The woman brought a male child into the world, the Son who was to rule all nations with an iron sceptre.

> *Rev. 12:1, 5. There is a musical setting of these words by*
> *Charles-Marie Widor (1844-1937).*

AVE MARIA

AVE Maria, gratia plena, Dominus tecum, benedicta tu in mulieribus et benedictus fructus ventris tui, Jesu. Sancta Maria, sancta Maria, Maria, ora pro nobis, nobis peccatoribus, nunc et in hora, in hora mortis nostrae. Amen. Amen.

> *Latin words adapted to fit the First Prelude by J. S. Bach (1685-1750).*
> *There is also a setting by Sergei Rachmaninov, in which the line "Sancta Maria, sancta Maria, Maria" is replaced by "Sancta Maria, mater Dei."*
> *Bach was in a Lutheran tradition, Rachmaninov in a Russian Orthodox one.*

AVE Maria!
Grace shall leave thee never.
God is with thee ever.
Blessed, shall thy name in ages be.
And blessed be thy holy Son,
Jesus, God and Man in one.
Hear us Mother, hear us when we cry to thee.
Sancta Maria!
Sancta Maria! Maria!
When this earthly life is past,
And our eyelids close at last,
Pray for us for ever,
For thy children ever.
Amen!

Ave Maria!
Mother pure and holy,
Sorrowful and lowly,
Blessed shall thy name for ever be.
For thou art ever near us,
Thou wilt ever hear us.
Aid us, Mother,
Aid us when we cry to thee.
Sancta Maria!
Sancta Maria! Maria!
Dearest Mother hear our prayer,
Take us in thy loving care.
Pray for us for ever,
For thy children ever pray.
Amen! Amen!

English version by Lionel Mundy
of the setting by Charles Gounod (1818-93)

Ave Maria!
Mighty, yet lowly,
Pure, and most holy,
Hear from thy starry throne our prayer:
Though faithless friends may grieve us,
Wealth and fortune leave us,
Grant to our grief and to our pain
Thy tender care.
Sancta Maria!
Sancta Maria! Maria!
When we are tearful,
When we are fearful,
Give to us thine aid,
To us thine aid,
Thine aid of prayer!

Ave Maria!
Mother of the desolate!
Guide of the unfortunate!
Hear from thy starry throne our prayer:
If sorrow will await us,
Tyrants vex and hate us,
Teach us thine own most patient part to bear!
Sancta Maria!
Sancta Maria! Maria!
When we are sighing,
When we are dying,
Give to us thine aid,
To us thine aid, thine aid of prayer!
Amen. Amen.

English transcription of the Gounod setting from
The Walsh Collection *(Fentone Music)*

HYMN: MARY IMMACULATE

"Himmels-Lust" (1679)
Leibster Immanuel   11 10. 11 10.   *adapted by J. S. Bach*

MARY Immaculate, Star of the morning,
Chosen before the creation began,
Chosen to bring, for thy bridal adorning,
Woe to the serpent and rescue to man.

Here, in an orbit of shadow and sadness,
Veiling thy splendour, thy course thou hast run;
Now thou art crowned in all glory and gladness,
Crowned by the hand of thy Saviour and Son.

147

Sinners, we worship thy sinless perfection;
Fallen and weak, for thy pity we plead;
Grant us the shield of thy sovereign perfection,
Measure thine aid by the depth of our need.

Frail is our nature and strict our probation,
Watchful the foe that would lead us to wrong:
Succour our souls in the hour of temptation,
Mary immaculate, tender and strong.

See how the wiles of the serpent assail us,
See how we waver and flinch in the fight;
Let thine immaculate merit avail us,
Make of our weakness a proof of thy might.

Bend from thy throne at the voice of our crying,
Bend to this earth which thy footsteps have trod;
Stretch out thine arms to us living and dying,
Mary Immaculate, Mother of God.

F. W. Weatherell

PRAYER

I dwell in the highest,
and my throne is on the pillar of the clouds.
O Lady, hear my prayer,
and let my cry come unto you.

BALLAD: FROM THE RELIEF OF BELGRADE

Now, Mary, mayden, helpe me todaye,
Or elles thy matyns shall I never saye
Dayes of all my lyve,
Ne no prayer that the shall please
But yf thou helpe now our desease,
Ne menye thy joyes fyve.
A poynt is for thy mayden hede

148

That all this people suffreth dede—
Now helpe to stynte our stryve!
Now, lady, of thy men have pyte,
Praye for them to thy sone on hye,
As thou arte mayden and wyfe!

Capystranus, late medieval

menye=commemoration, mention
dede=death   A poynt is=it is because of

PRAYER TO THE BLESSED VIRGIN MARY

MOST Holy and Immaculate Virgin and my Mother
Mary, to you who are the Mother of my Lord, the Queen
of the world, the advocate, the hope, and the refuge of
sinners I, who am the most miserable of all, have recourse
this day. I render you my most humble homage, O great
Queen, and I thank you for all the graces you have
obtained for me until now, especially for having saved me
from hell, which I have so often deserved. I love you,
most amiable Lady, and because of the love which I bear
you I promise to serve you always and to do all in my
power to make others love you also. In you I place all my
hopes; to you I entrust the salvation of my soul. Accept
me as your servant, and receive me under your mantle, O
Mother of Mercy; and since you are so powerful with
God, deliver me from all temptations, or rather obtain for
me the strength to triumph over them until death. I ask
of you a true love for Jesus Christ; from you I hope to
obtain the grace of a holy death. O my Mother, by the
love which you bear to God, I ask you to help me at all
times, but especially at the last moment of my life. Do
not leave me until you see me safe in heaven, where I shall
bless you and sing your mercies through all eternity.

Amen, so I hope, so may it be.

HYMN: O GLORIOSA VIRGINUM

Wells   L.M.   *European Psalmist (1872)*

QUEEN, on whose starry brow doth rest
The crown of perfect maidenhood,
The God who made thee, from thy breast,
Drew, for our sakes, his earthly food.

The grace that sinful Eve denied,
With thy child-bearing, reappears;
Heaven's lingering door, set open wide,
Welcomes the children of her tears.

Gate, for such royal progress meet,
Beacon, whose rays such light can give,
Look, how the ransomed nations greet
The virgin-womb that bade them live!

O Jesus, whom the Virgin bore,
Be praise and glory unto thee;
Praise to the Father evermore
And his life-giving Spirit be.

Venantius Fortunatus (530-609). Trans. R. A. Knox

The Birthday of Our Lady

Like other feasts of Our Lady, this one originated in the East. It was known in the West by the middle of the seventh century. Pope Sergius I (687-701) ordered it to be celebrated in Rome and marked by a procession, along with the feasts of the Annunciation, the Purification and the Assumption.

There is nothing said in the Bible about Mary's birth, and her parents, traditionally known as SS Joachim and Anne, appear only in Apocryphal Gospels. The story is that they had long been childless; Joachim withdrew into the desert to lament this fate and there learned in a dream that he and Anne would soon have a daughter. An old tradition accepted in the West makes Nazareth Mary's birthplace, though other traditions favour Jerusalem, near the pool of Bethsaida, where a small oratory existed from early in the third century, in a crypt under the church of St Anne. In the Georgian Calendar of Jerusalem, compiled in the seventh or eighth century, it had become, with the Annunciation, one of the two principal feasts of Our Lady.

It is not known why the date of 8 September was chosen, but the feast provides another opportunity for Christians to reflect on Mary's unique place in the history of salvation.

Condensed from Butler's Lives of the Saints, *September volume*

On 8 September 994 the people of London prayed to Our Blessed Lady to protect them from the Viking attack. The well-known nursery rhyme refers to this:

> London Bridge
> is falling down,

falling down, falling down,
My Fair Lady.

My Fair Lady is Our Blessed Lady

LITANY OF THE BLACK VIRGIN *(from the French)*

Lord, have mercy upon us.
  Jesus Christ, have mercy upon us.
Jesus Christ, hear us.
  Jesus Christ, hear our prayer.
God the Father, creator,
  have mercy upon us.
God the Son, redeemer,
  have mercy upon us.
God the Holy Spirit, sanctifier,
  have mercy upon us.
Holy Trinity, which is One God,
  have mercy upon us.

Holy Mary,   *pray for us. (After each invocation)*
Virgin, queen and patron;
Virgin, whom Zacchaeus the publican
  made us know and love;
Virgin, to whom Zacchaeus or St Amadour
  constructed this shrine;
Queen of this shrine, which St Martial consecrated
  and at which he celebrated his holy mysteries;
Queen, before whom St Louis knelt to pray
  for the good fortune of France;
Queen, whose banner won battles;
Queen, whose hand delivered the captives;
Our Lady, whose pilgrimage is blessed
  with special favours;

152

Our Lady, whom impiety and hatred
  have often sought to destroy;
Our Lady, whom the people visit as in former times;
Lamb of God, who takest away the sins of the world,
  forgive us.
Lamb of God, who takest away the sins of the world,
  hear our prayer.
Lamb of God, who takest away the sins of the world,
  have mercy upon us.
Our Lady, pray for us,
  that we may be worthy of Jesus Christ.

*According to legend, the wooden statue of Our Lady at the shrine of
Rocamadour had been carved by St Amadour. Nothing is known
about him, but he was identified in popular legend with Zacchaeus
the publican (see Luke 19:1-10), who was married to Veronica and
was a friend of St Peter. Pilgrims on the way to Santiago de
Compostela flocked to Rocamadour largely because of its reputation
for miracles (see M. Walsh,* A Dictionary of Devotions, *p. 219).*

  *The French text of this litany has been set to music by François
Poulenc (1899-1963), as part of his Mass in G.*

HIGH MASS
ON THE FEAST OF THE NATIVITY OF OUR LADY
*Selected texts used in the setting by Guillaume de Machaut
(fourteenth century)*

INTROIT

GAUDEAMUS omnes in Domino
diem festum celebrantes sub honore Mariae virginis
de cuius nativitate gaudent angeli
et collaudant Filium Dei.

153

Eructavit cor meum verbum bonum:
dico ego opera mea regi.
Gaudeamus omnes in Domino...
Gloria Patri, et Filio, et Spiritui Sancto:
Sicut erat in principio, et nunc, et semper,
et in saecula saeculorum, Amen.
Gaudeamus omnes in Domino . . .

Let us all rejoice in the Lord
as we keep a feast-day in honour of the Virgin Mary,
whose birth makes angels rejoice
and sets them praising the Son of God.
My heart overflows with a goodly theme:
I address my poem to the King.
Let us all rejoice in the Lord...
Glory be... Amen.
Let us all rejoice in the Lord ...

GRADUAL AND ALLELUIA

Audi filia et vide et inclina aurem tuam
quia concupivit rex speciem tuam.
Specie tua et pulchritudine tua intende
prospere procede et regna.
Alleluia, alleluia.
Nativitas gloriosae Virginis Mariae
ex semine Abrahae
orta de tribu Juda clara ex stirpe David.
Alleluia.

Hear, O daughter, consider, and incline your ear,
for the King has desired your beauty.
With your grace and with your beauty be resolved,
set forth with good fortune and reign.

Alleluia, alleluia!
The nativity of the glorious Virgin Mary
descended from the seed of Abraham,
of the noble tribe of Judah and from the stock of David.
Alleluia!

SEQUENCE

Hac clara die turma festiva dat praeconia
Maria concrepando simphonia nestarea:
Mundi domina quae est sola castissima virginum regina,
Salutis causa, vitae porta atque caeli refecta gratia,
Nam ad illam sic nuntia olim facta angelica:
Ave Maria, gratia plena per saecula.
Mulierum pia agmina intra semper benedicta,
Virgo et mater gravida intacta, prole gloriosa.
Cui contra Maria haec reddit famina,
In me quomodo tuo iam fient nuntia?
Viri novi nullam certe copulam
Ex quo atque nata sum incorrupta.
Quia missus ita redit affata:
Flatu sacro plena fies Maria,
Nova efferens gaudia caelo terrae nati per exordia,
Intro tui uteri claustra portans qui gubernat aeterna,
Omnia qui dat tempora pacifica. Amen

On this bright day the festive throng gives praise
And calls to Mary in sweetest harmony:
The world's Lady and virgins' most chaste Queen,
Salvation's cause, life's gateway, heaven's refreshing grace,
To whom the angelic greeting once was made:
"Hail Mary, of God's grace ever full,
Ever blessed among the holy band of women,
Pure maiden, fruitful Mother, made glorious by your child."
To whom the Virgin returned this reply:

155

"How can there be in me the things you tell?
For surely I am innocent of man,
And my birth was itself immaculate."
The messenger made answer with these words:"You shall be
filled with the Spirit's holy breath,
Bringing new joy to heaven by the Son's birth in the world,
Carrying safe in your womb Him who governs eternity,
Who gives all periods of peace." Amen.

> *Introt, Gradual and Alleluia translated by David Evans;*
> *Sequence by Nick Sandon*

BENEDICTA ET VENERABILIS ES: GRADUAL

Benedicta et venerabilis es,
sacra Virgo Maria,
quae sine tactu pudoris inventa es
mater Salvatoris.
There is a musical setting by William Byrd (c. 1543-1623).

You are blessed and worthy to be revered,
Mary, holy Virgin,
who without a touch of shame were found to be
the Saviour's Mother.

MEDITATION

Following the study of Sacred Scripture, the Fathers, the
doctors and liturgy of the Church, and under the guidance of the Church's magisterium, let [theologians and
preachers of the Word of God] rightly illustrate the duties
and privileges of the Blessed Virgin which always refer to
Christ, the source of all truth, sanctity, and devotion.

Second Vatican Council, Lumen Gentium, *67.*

156

PRAYER *(A Novena prayer for priests and religious)*

O MARY, who wert promised from the beginning to crush the serpent's head, and to bring forth the Redeemer of mankind, in thy birth appeared the dawn of that glorious day of grace, for which all nations ardently sighed.

O happy Virgin, who, on entering the world, didst become a victim of charity, perfectly and unreservedly submissive to the will of God; may we be enriched with a share in the dispositions with which thy soul was adorned in thy earliest infancy: inspire us by thy example and intercession with that spirit of renunciation, self-contempt, and detachment from the world, which we promised at our baptism, and which we more solemnly engaged ourselves to practise at our profession.

We conjure thee, O Immaculate Virgin, by the purity and sanctity of thy nativity, and by the riches of grace and virtue which the weakness of childhood then concealed in thee, to obtain for us the intentions of this Novena....

Obtain for us, also, strength to fulfil the duties of our exalted vocation, to co-operate with the graces of heaven, and to advance faithfully towards that perfection to which we are bound to aspire. Amen.

Choir manual of the Little Office of the B.V.M.,
recited after Vespers from 30 August to 8 September

PRAYER *(Traditional)*

> MARY, purest flower of earth,
> Mary, gate of heaven,
> Mary, who to nature's dearth
> Mercy's fount hast given;
> Mary, Queen of virtues rarest,
> Mary, who salvation barest,
> Mary, house with treasures stored,
> Lead me to my King adored.

15 September
Our Lady of Sorrows

Our Lady traditionally suffered seven sorrows during her life. The list of these has varied over the centuries, but in the form generally accepted they are:

(i) Simeon's prophecy of Mary's heart being pierced; (ii) the flight into Egypt; (iii) the loss of the child Jesus in the temple; (iv) Mary meets Jesus on the way to Calvary; (v) Mary stands at the foot of the cross during the crucifixion; (vi) Jesus is taken down from the cross and placed in the arms of his mother; (vii) the burial of Jesus.

This order was established in the late fourteenth century. The feast of the Seven Sorrows (or Dolours) was extended to the whole Church by Pius VII in 1814 in thanksgiving for his return to Rome after being held captive in France. It was then observed on the Friday before Palm Sunday and was moved to 15 September in 1913. In the Calendar reform of 1969 it was renamed Our Lady of Sorrows and ranked as an obligatory memorial.

The figure of the sorrowing mother at the foot of the cross has inspired painters, poets and musicians down through the ages. The best-known result is the hymn "Stabat mater" (for the Latin text see pp. 69-71).

HYMN: STABAT MATER

> AT the cross her station keeping,
> Stood the mournful Mother weeping,
> Close to Jesus to the last.
>
> Through her heart, his sorrow sharing,
> All his bitter anguish bearing,
> Lo! the piercing sword had passed.
>
> O how sad and sore distressed
> Was that Mother, highly blessed,
> Of the sole-begotten One.
>
> Jesus, may thy cross defend me,
> And thy Mother's prayer befriend me;
> Let me die in thy embrace.
>
> When to dust my dust returneth,
> Grant a soul that to thee yearneth,
> In thy paradise a place.
>
> Amen.

PRAYER OF ST BONAVENTURE *(thirteenth century)*

What tongue can tell, what intellect grasp
the heavy weight of your desolation, blessed Virgin?
You were present at all these events, standing close by
and participating in them in every way.

Gradual and Alleluia from the Mass

Dolorosa et lacrimabilis es, Virgo Maria, stans juxta crucem Domini Jesu Filii tui Redemptoris.

℣. Virgo Dei Genitrix, quem totus non capit orbis, hoc crucis fert supplicium, auctor vitae factus homo.

Alleluia, Alleluia!

℣. Stabat Sancta Maria, caeli Regina et mundi Domina, juxta crucem Domini nostri Jesu Christi dolorosa.

Mary, Virgin, broken-hearted and weeping you stand close to the cross of your Son, Jesus Christ, our Lord and Redeemer.

℣. Virgin Mother of God, the whole world cannot contain him, yet he, the author of life, became a man, and this gibbet, the cross, now bears him.

Alleluia, Alleluia!

℣. She stood there close to the cross of our Lord Jesus Christ, his holy mother, the queen of heaven and empress of the world, bowed down with grief.

Layman's Missal and Prayer Book (1962)

Hymn: The Seven Dolours of Our Lady

Pendens in crucis cornibus
  Longe porrectis manibus
Ob genitricis merita
  Trahe nos ad celestia.

Quam prope stantem caritas
  Plaga doloris penetras,
Fac, pia, nos in pectore
  Hoc sauciare vulnere.

SUMMER

Tu sol occasum nesciens
    Mortem qui vincis moriens,
Piae parentis precibus
    Nostris appare mentibus.

Virgo, quae unigenitum
    Tuum plorasti mortuum,
Da pietatis lacrymas
    Nostrasque dele maculas.

Verum Joseph in tumulum
    Christi ponunt corpusculum,
Matris obtentu, Kyrie,
    Nos morte victa redime.

Stella maris praefulgida,
    Ad viam vitae praevia,
Exutos carnis pondere
    In Christi fac quiescere.

Custos tuarum ovium,
    Quam turma servat militum,
Ab omni nos temptamine
    Matris oratu protege.

Regina caeli Maria
    Quam laudat omnis anima,
Completo nos servitio,
    Remuneret donatio.

Gloria tibi, Domine,
    Qui natus es de virgine,
Cum Patre et Sancto Spiritu
    In sempiterna saecula.

MAIDEN AND MOTHER

O thou who hangest on the tree
*   With arms wide-stretched in charity,*
Grant us at thy blest Mother's prayer
*   To meet thee on the heavenly stair.*

Love, and a sevenfold sorrow's dart
*   Beside the cross tranfixed thy heart;*
Lady of mercy, grant to us
*   To share that wound most dolorous.*

Jesu, thou sun that know'st no night,
*   That conquerest death by death's own might,*
Unto thy servants' hearts appear
*   Now at thy blissful Mother's prayer.*

Maiden, who weepest for thy Son,
*   The blessed Sole-begotten One,*
Grant us the tears of love, we pray,
*   And wash our every stain away.*

The God she bare within her womb
*   Is laid within the rock-hewn tomb;*
Our souls enchained by death of yore,
*   Lord, at thy Mother's prayer restore.*

Star of the Sea most fair, we pray,
*   That guid'st us on life's narrow way,*
No more by bonds of flesh oppressed,
*   Grant us in Christ thy Son to rest.*

O Shepherd of the sheep, thy praise
*   A thousand bands of angels raise;*
From all temptation thine elect
*   At thy blest Mother's prayer protect.*

Queen in the land of starshining
Whose praises every heart doth sing,
When all our earthly praise is done,
Reward us with thy benison.

Glory to thee through all the earth,
Lord Jesu, for thy virgin birth,
With Father and with Spirit one
While endless ages onward run.

Found in MSS of Polish and Bohemian hymnaries
of the fourteenth century

AVE MARIA

Hail Mary!
Virgin of heaven,
Queen of grace and holy Mother,
Receive a fervent prayer,
Do not deny my bewildered heart
Relief in its distress!
My lost soul turns to you,
And at your feet, full of hope,
Implores you and awaits the sweet peace
That only you can give.
Hail Mary!

Hail Mary!
Full of grace,
Mary, full of grace.
Hail, hail, the Lord is with thee.
Blessed art thou among women,
And blessed, blessed is the fruit of thy womb, Jesus.
Hail Mary!

Version of the German set to music by Franz Schubert (1799-1828)

Hymn: The Seven Sorrows

Nun komm ...   *77.77.*   *Walther's Gesangbüchlein (1524)*

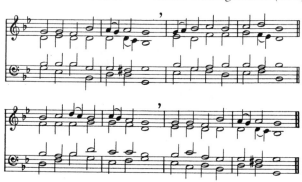

God in whom all grace doth dwell!
Grant us grace to ponder well
On the Virgin's dolours seven,
On the wounds to Jesus given.

May the tears which Mary poured
Gain us pardon of the Lord—
Tears excelling in their worth
All the penances of earth.

May the contemplation sore
Of the wounds which Jesus bore,
Source to us of blessings be
Through a long eternity.

Ascribed to Callisto Palunabella (18th century)
Trans. Edward Caswall (1814-78)

24 September (in England and Wales)
Our Lady of Ransom

This title is associated with the appearance in 1233 of Our Lady to St Peter Nolasco (25 December), regarded as the chief founder of the Mercedarian Order, founded in Spain to ransom Christian slaves from the Muslims. Under this title Our Lady is principal patron of Barcelona, with a shrine in the cathedral. Before the 1969 Calendar reform it was a feast of the universal Church, but is now for local observance in Spain and England and Wales.

The English connection stems from the founding of the Guild of Our Lady of Ransom, founded in 1887 by Fr Philip Fletcher and Lister Drummond, converts from Anglicanism, who saw a parallel between the medieval ransomers and the task of converting England back to Catholicism. Pope Leo XIII blessed the Guild and became its first Protector, a tradition continued by all subsequent popes. It supports missions in poor areas of England and Wales, and the Sunday closest to 24 September is observed as Home Mission Sunday.

COLLECT FOR THE FEAST OF OUR LADY OF RANSOM

O GOD, who, under the protection of the glorious Mother of thy Son, wast pleased that the Order of Mercy should be instituted in thy Church, for the relief of suffering and instruction of the ignorant; vouchsafe so to strengthen and enlighten those to whom thou hast granted this holy vocation, that they may faithfully and efficaciously dispense thy mercies on earth, and thereby come to the enjoyment of thy divine presence in heaven, through Jesus Christ our Lord. Amen.

From the Little Office of the B.V.M.
Said as part of a Novena from 16 to 24 September.

165

PRAYER

Heavenly Father
who from the very birth of the Church in our land,
did make us the dowry of Mary
and loyal subjects of the Prince of the Apostles;
grant us your grace
to continue steadfast in the Catholic faith,
ever devoted to the Virgin Mary as our Mother
and ever faithful
in our allegiance to the See of Peter.
Amen.

PRAYER OF ST GERTRUDE THE GREAT
FOR INCREASE OF FAITH

HAIL, MARY, queen of mercy, olive-branch of forgiveness, through whom we receive the medicine that heals
our mortal sickness, the balsam of pardon: Virgin Mother
of the divine offspring, through whom the grace of heavenly light has been shed upon us, the sweet-scented scion
of Israel!

Through they Son, thy only Child who stooped to
become the Brother of mankind, thou art become the
true Mother of us all. For the sake of his love take me, all
unworthy as I am, into thy motherly care. Sustain, preserve, and enlighten my conversion; be thou for all eternity my incomparable cherished mother, tenderly caring
for me throughout my earthly life, and enfolding me in
thy arms at the hour of my death. Amen.

HYMN: *O maid conceived without a stain*

> O MAID conceived without a stain,
> O Mother bright and fair,
> Come thou within our hearts to reign
> And grace shall triumph there.
> *Hail Mary ever undefiled,*
> *Hail, Queen of purity,*
> *O make thy children chaste and mild*
> *And turn their hearts to thee.*

> O Mother of all mothers best
> Who soothest every grief,
> In thee the weary find their rest
> And anguished hearts relief.
> *Hail Mary ever...*

Traditional

Our Lady's Saturdays

PRAYERS TO BE SAID IN THE MORNINGS

> Mary, my dear Mother,
> how much I love you!
> And yet in reality how little!
> You teach me what I ought to know,
> for you teach me what Jesus is to me
> and what I ought to be for Jesus.

> Dearly beloved Mother, how close to God you are,
> and how utterly filled with him!
> In the measure that we know God,
> we remind ourselves of you.
> Mother of God,
> obtain for me the grace of loving my Jesus;
> obtain for me the grace of loving you!

Cardinal Rafael Merry del Val (1865-1930)

167

Holy Mary, be a mother to me.
Angels and saints of God, pray for me.

FROM THE MASS

Gradual and Alleluia

BLESSED art thou, and worshipful, Mary, Virgin; who without loss of maidenhood wast found to be the Mother of our Saviour.

Virgin Mother of God, he whom the entire world cannot hold enclosed himself within thy womb and was made man.

Alleluia, alleluia. Thou didst bear a child, still keeping thy virginity unspoiled: Mother of God, plead for us. Alleluia.

Gospel Reading

As Jesus was speaking to the crowd, a woman in the multitude said to him aloud: "Blessed is the womb that bore thee, the breast which thou hast sucked." And he answered: "Shall we not say, Blessed are they who hear the word of God, and keep it?" *Luke 11:27-8*

PRAYERS

> AVE Maria, gratia plena,
> Dominus tecum;
> Benedicta tu in mulieribus,
> et benedictus fructis ventris tui, Jesus.
> Sancta Maria, Mater Dei,
> ora pro nobis peccatoribus,
> nunc et in hora mortis nostrae. Amen

Musical settings of the Latin text of the "Hail Mary" include one by Sir Edward Elgar, his Opus 2/2 (1887), and another by Anton Bruckner (1824-96).

SUMMER

O thou Mother! fount of love,
　　Touch my spirit from above;
Make my heart with thine accord:
　　Make me feel as thou hast felt;
Make my soul to glow and melt
　　With the love of Christ my Lord.

From the hymn Stabat Mater

MOTET: *Tota Pulchra Es*

Tota pulchra es, Maria,
et macula originalis non est in te.
Vestimentum tuum candidum quasi nix,
et facies tua sicut sol.
Tu gloria Jerusalem,
tu laetitia Israel,
tu honorificentia populi nostri.

Thou art all beauty, Mary,
and there is no blemish of original sin in thee.
Thy garments are as white as snow
and thy face is as the sun.
Thou art the glory of Jerusalem,
the joy of Israel,
the source of honour to our people.

Based on The Song of Songs 4:7 and Judith 15:10.
There is a musical setting by Maurice Duruflé (b. 1902),
Motet sur des thèmes grégoriens.

169

HYMN: *Ye who own the Faith of Jesus*

> YE who own the faith of Jesus
> Sing the wonders that were done,
> When the love of God the Father
> O'er our sin the victory won,
> When he made the Virgin Mary
> Mother of his only Son.
> *Hail, Mary full of grace.*
>
> Blessed were the chosen people
> Out of whom the Lord did come,
> Blessed was the land of promise
> Fashioned for his earthly home;
> But more blessed far the Mother,
> She who bore him in her womb.
> *Hail, Mary, full of grace.*
>
> Wherefore let all faithful people
> Tell the honour of her name,
> Let the Church in her foreshadowed
> Part in her thanksgiving claim;
> What Christ's Mother sang in gladness
> Let Christ's people sing the same.
> *Hail, Mary, full of grace.*
>
> May the Mother's intercessions
> On our homes a blessing win,
> That the children all be prospered
> Strong and fair and pure within,
> Following Our Lord's own footsteps,
> Firm in faith and free from sin.
> *Hail, Mary, full of grace.*

For the sick and for the aged,
For our dear ones far away,
For the hearts that mourn in secret,
All who need our prayers today,
For the faithful gone before us,
May the holy Virgin pray.
Hail, Mary, full of grace.

Praise, O Mary, praise the Father,
Praise thy Saviour and thy Son,
Praise the everlasting Spirit,
Who hath made thee ark and throne.
O'er all creatures high exalted,
Lowly praise the Three in One.
Hail, Mary, full of grace.

V.S.S. Coles (1845-1929)

※

PRAYER OF ST JOHN BOSCO
TO OUR LADY HELP OF CHRISTIANS

O MARY, powerful Virgin, thou mighty and glorious
protector of holy Church; thou marvellous help of
Christians; thou who art awe-inspiring as an army in
battle array; thou by whom alone all heresies throughout
the world are brought to nothing: in our anguish, our
struggles, our distress, guard us from the enemy's power,
and at the hour of our death bid our souls welcome into
paradise. Amen.

171

HYMN:*Look down, O Mother Mary*

Vaughan   76.76.D.   *J. Richardson, 1816-79 (A.G.M.)*

LOOK down, O Mother Mary,
From thy bright throne above;
Cast down upon thy children
One only glance of love;
And if a heart so tender
With pity flows not o'er,
Then turn away, O Mother,
And look on us no more.

SUMMER

Look down, O Mother Mary,
From thy bright throne above;
Cast down upon thy children
One only glance of love.

See how, ungrateful sinners,
We stand before thy Son;
His loving heart upbraids us
The evil we have done,
But if thou wilt appease him,
Speak for us but one word;
For thus thou canst obtain us
The pardon of our Lord.

Look down, O Mother Mary,
From thy bright throne above;
Cast down upon thy children
One only glance of love.

O Mary, dearest Mother,
If thou wouldst have us live,
Say that we are thy children,
And Jesus will forgive.
Our sins make us unworthy
That title still to bear,
But thou art still our Mother:
Then show a mother's care.

Look down, O Mother Mary,
From thy bright throne above;
Cast down upon thy children
One only glance of love.

MAIDEN AND MOTHER

Unfold to us thy mantle,
There stay we without fear;
What evil can befall us
If, Mother, thou art near?
O kindest, dearest Mother,
Thy sinful people save;
Look down on us with pity,
Who thy protection crave.

Look down, O Mother Mary,
From thy bright throne above;
Cast down upon thy children
One only glance of love.

"Dal tuo celeste" by St Alphonsus Liguori (1696-1787)
Trans. Edward Vaughan (1827-1908)

ORDINARY TIME II

AUTUMN

*This Autumn period covers from the beginning of October
to the beginning of Advent.
Celebrations of Our Lady during this period include
Our Lady of the Rosary on 7 October and
The Presentation of Our Lady on 21 November.*

*Traditionally, the month of October is devoted to the Rosary.
As most of November falls in Ordinary Time, the Mass and
Morning Office of Our Lady can be celebrated on Saturdays
unless a solemnity, feast, or obligatory memorial
falls on that particular Saturday.*

*A pilgrimage prayer and hymn to Our Lady of
Walsingham, the popular shrine in Norfolk,
have been included in this section.*

*The liturgical colour for the season is green,
with white on Our Lady of the Rosary and
The Presentation of Our Lady.*

THE CROWNING OF OUR LADY IN HEAVEN
*(see following page and also The Queenship of Mary,
pages 144–50)*

7 October
Our Lady of the Rosary

The Dominican Order of Friars Preachers, also known as Black Friars from their black habit worn over a full-length white garment, was formally confirmed by Pope Honorius III on 22 December1216. These friars combine the contemplative life of monks with the active life of the secular clergy. They were to be the most influential advocates of devotion to the Rosary and established confraternities of the Rosary, who were the first to observe this feast.

Its date was originally established as the first Sunday in October, in thanksgiving for the victory of the Christian forces over the Turks at the battle of Lepanto on 7 October 1571, which was the first Sunday of the month. This date had long been celebrated by the Rosary confraternities, and the victory was widely attributed to Our Lady of the Rosary. Pope Gregory XIII allowed it to be celebrated in any church that had a Rosary confraternity in 1573, and it became a feast for the whole Church in 1716, in thanksgiving for another victory over the Turks. In 1913 the date was established as that of the actual date of Lepanto rather than the first Sunday in October.

The name "Rosary" comes from rosarium, *meaning a garland of white roses worn on the head. The rose is a symbol of joy, so the Rosary is a message of joy. It is prayed on a set of beads made up of five lots of ten, on each of which a* Hail Mary *is prayed, with an intervening* Our Father *preceding each batch of ten or "decad."and a* Glory be... *following. Each decade commemorates a "mystery" associated with Our Lord's life, five joyful, five sorrowful, and five glorious, so in all 150* Hail Marys *are said, a number corresponding to the 150*

Psalms of the Divine Office. By the middle of the thirteenth century it was referred to as the "psalter of Saint Mary." The fifteen "mysteries" had become constant by the end of the fifteenth century. The apparitions at Lourdes, where the Virgin appeared holding a rosary, gave fresh impetus to the devotion. New forms of devotion such as the Month of the Rosary and the Rosary Crusade have ensured its lasting popularity, and it is increasingly used outside the Roman Catholic Church.

The Five Joyful Mysteries of the Rosary are:

> The Annunciation
> The Visitation
> The Nativity
> The Presentation of Jesus in the Temple
> The Finding of Jesus in the Temple.

These are prayed on Mondays and Thursdays.

The Five Sorrowful Mysteries are:

> The Agony in the Garden
> The Scourging at the Pillar
> The Crowning with Thorns
> The Carrying of the Cross
> The Crucifixion.

These are prayed on Tuesdays and Fridays.

The Five Glorious Mysteries are:

> The Resurrection
> The Ascension
> The Descent of the Holy Spirit on the Apostles
> The Assumption of Our Lady into Heaven
> The Crowning of Our Lady in Heaven.

These are prayed on Wednesdays, Saturdays, and Sundays.

Mystery means truth, and these mysteries are meditations on truths of Our Lord's life from his birth as a human baby to his death and glory with the Father in heaven. Mary is associated with these mysteries, and watches over us as a loving

Mother as we pray the Rosary with and through her. The title of each mystery should be stated at the beginning of each decade of the Rosary and the truth it represents should be contemplated during the saying of that decade. Begin and end each Rosary with the sign of the cross and on the five beads below the medallion say the Apostles' Creed, *three* Hail Marys, *and the concluding prayer* Sub tuum praesidium, *(the earliest known prayer to Our Lady–see below) or* Salve Regina, *"Hail, Holy Queen," which is often preferred today.*

In the shadow of your mercy we shelter
O holy Mother of God,
Do not ignore our petitions in our needs,
But keep us safe from all dangers,
O ever-virgin, glorious and blessed

A SCRIPTURE ROSARY

There are several possible ways of praying the rosary. A scriptural "long form" would use a verse or part of a verse from the scriptures before each prayer. This may be either spoken out loud in a group or read silently. Here, for reasons of space, a "short form" is given, with a verse or short passage applied to each mystery.

First Joyful Mystery: The Annunciation

In the sixth month, the angel Gabriel was sent from God to a city of Galilee named Nazareth, to a virgin betrothed to a man whose name was Joseph, of the house of David; and the virgin's name was Mary. *Luke 1:26-7*

Second Joyful Mystery: The Visitation

In those days Mary arose and went with haste into the hill

country, to a city of Judah, and she entered the house of Zechariah and greeted Elizabeth. And when Elizabeth heard the greeting of Mary, the babe leaped in her womb; and Elizabeth was filled with the Holy Spirit....*Luke 1:39-41*

Third Joyful Mystery: The Nativity
And while they were there, the time came for her to be delivered. And she gave birth to her first-born son and wrapped him in swaddling cloths, and laid him in a manger, because there was no room for them in the inn.
Luke 2:6-7

Fourth Joyful Mystery: The Presentation of Jesus in the Temple
And when the time came for their purification according to the law of Moses, they brought him up to Jerusalem to present him to the Lord (as it is written in the law of the Lord, "Every male that opens the womb shall be called holy to the Lord")....
Luke 2:22-4

Fifth Joyful Mystery: The Finding of Jesus in the Temple
After three days they found him in the temple, sitting among the teachers, listening to them and asking them questions; and all who heard him were amazed at his understanding and his answers.
Luke 2:46-7

First Sorrowful Mystery: The Agony in the Garden
Then Jesus went with them to a place called Gethsemane, and he said to his disciples, "Sit here, while I go yonder and pray." And taking with him Peter and the two sons of Zebedee, he began to be sorrowful and troubled.
Matt. 26:36-7

Second Sorrowful Mystery: The Scourging at the Pillar

180

Then Pilate took Jesus and scourged him. *John 19:1*

Third Sorrowful Mystery: the Crowning with Thorns
And the soldiers plaited a crown of thorns, and put it on his head. *John 19:2*

Fourth Sorrowful Mystery: The Carrying of the Cross
So they took Jesus, and he went out, bearing his own cross, to the place called the place of a skull, which is called in Hebrew Golgotha. *John 19:17*

Fifth Sorrowful Mystery: The Crucifixion
There they crucified him, and with him two others, one on either side, and Jesus between them. *John 19:18*

First Glorious Mystery: The Resurrection
Now on the first day of the week Mary Magdalene came to the tomb early, while it was still dark, and saw that the stone had been taken away from the tomb. So she ran, and went to Simon Peter and the other disciple, the one whom Hesus loved, and said to them, They have taken the Lord out of the tomb, and we do not know where they have laid him."...Then the other disciple, who reached the tomb first, also went in, and he saw and believed; for as yet they did not know the scripture, that he must rise from the dead. *John 20:1-2; 8-9*

Second Glorious Mystery: The Ascension
As they were looking on, he was lifted up, and a cloud took him out of their sight. And while they were gazing into heaven as he went, behold, two men stood by them in white robes, and said, "Men of Galilee, why do you stand looking into heaven? This Jesus, who was taken from you into heaven, will come in the same way as you

saw him go into heaven." *Acts 1:9-11*

Third Glorious Mystery: The Descent of the Holy Spirit on the Apostles

When the day of Pentecost had come, they were all together in one place. And suddenly a sound came from heaven like the rush of a mighty wind, and it filled all the house where they were sitting. And there appeared to them tongues as of fire, distributed and resting on each one of them. And they were all filled with the Holy Spirit and began to speak in other tongues, as the Spirit gave them utterance. *Acts 2:1-4*

Fourth Glorious Mystery: The Assumption of Our Lady into Heaven

"For he who is mighty has done great things for me, and holy is his name." *Luke 1:49*

Fifth Glorious Mystery: The Crowning of Our Lady in Heaven

And a great portent appeared in heaven, a woman clothed with the sun, with the moon under her feet, and on her head a crown of twelve stars.... *Rev. 12:1*

Repeat with appropriate verses for each of the mysteries.

182

HYMN: THE HOLY ROSARY *(Te gestientem gaudiis)*

St Gall.   L.M.   *Cantarium S. Galli, 1845*

THE gladness of thy motherhood,
The anguish of thy suffering,
The glory now that crowns thy brow,
O Virgin Mother, we would sing.

Hail, blessèd Mother, full of joy
In thy consent, thy visit too:
Joy in the birth of Christ on earth,
Joy in him lost and found anew.

Hail, sorrowing in his agony—
The blows, the thorns that pierced his brow;
The heavy wood, the shameful Rood—
Yea! Queen and chief of martyrs thou.

Hail, in the triumph of thy Son,
The quickening flames of Pentecost;
Shining as Queen in light serene,
When all the world is tempest-tost.

O come, ye nations, roses bring,
Culled from these mysteries divine,

And for the Mother of your King
With loving hands your chaplets twine.
We lay our homage at thy feet,
Lord Jesus, thou the Virgin's Son,
With Father and with Paraclete,
Reigning while endless ages run.

Trans. from the Marquess of Bute's Breviary
by Augustine Rucchini, O.P. (18th century)

PRAYERS AND HYMNS FOR THE MONTH OF OCTOBER—ROSARY MONTH

Prayers from Dawn to Night, from the Little Office of the Immaculate Conception, may be said again throughout October; they will be found under Our Lady's Month, in the Pentecost section, pages 87–96.

AN OPENING PRAYER

HOLY Mary, Queen of heaven, Mother of our Lord Jesus Christ and of his Church, who forsakes no one and despises no one, look upon me with an eye of pity, and entreat for me of your beloved Son the forgiveness of all my sins: that, as I now celebrate with affection your holy and immaculate conception, so hereafter, I may receive the prize of eternal blessedness, by the grace of him whom you, in virginity, brought forth,
Jesus Christ our Lord:
who, with the Father and the Holy Spirit,
lives and reigns, in perfect Trinity.
God, for ever and ever,

184

Amen.

Our Lady of Walsingham

In 1061 a noblewoman of Norfolk named Richeldis de Faverches, was supposedly instructed in three visions of the Virgin Mary to build an exact copy of the holy house in Nazareth in which the Annunciation had taken place. The following night she found that angels had built the house and moved it to a new site, where two springs of water appeared. Walsingham, on this basis, became one of the great pilgrimage destinations of the Middle Ages. The wooden structure (which in fact probably dated from the mid-twelfth century) was burned down at the Reformation. In 1863 Miss Charlotte Boyd bought the building known as the "slipper chapel" about a mile south of Walsingham. She became a Catholic and made the building over to the Benedictines. The first modern pilgrimage took place in 1897. An Anglican parish priest built a church on the site of what was thought to be the original house, and Walsingham is today a major focus of inter-denominational pilgrimage.

AN ANCIENT PRAYER TO OUR LADY OF WALSINGHAM

O ALONE of all women, Mother and Virgin, Mother most happy, Virgin most pure, now we, sinful as we are, come to see thee who art all pure. We salute thee, we honour thee as how we may with our humble offerings; may thy Son grant us, that imitating thy most holy manners, we also, by the grace of the Holy Spirit, may deserve spiritually to conceive the Lord Jesus in our inmost soul, and once conceived never to lose him. Amen.

MAIDEN AND MOTHER

Attributed to Desiderius Erasmus (1466-1536)

A PILGRIMAGE HYMN *To Our Lady of Walsingham*
Walsingham   D.L.M.   A.G.M.
UNISON

> HERE journeyed, on the Pilgrims' Way,
> With Christendom in youth and flower,
> The faithful of a happier day
> When all the land was Mary's dower.
> And after many a faithless year,
> Since not in vain the martyrs sowed,
> We, as God wills, to worship here
> Return along the ancient road.

Once more with invocation due,
Lady, thy solemn names ascend,
While for thy prayer we ask anew
To guard our days and bless our end.
Maiden most humble, angels' Queen,
Mother and handmaid of the Lord,
Of God's design the goal foreseen,
Fountain of hope and love's reward.

Thou, by the grace of God thy Son
Our pillar and our ground of grace,
Perfect in us the work begun
And sanctify the rescued race.
In worldly storm, in stress of ill,
Be thou the star that lights our sea;
Keep us in courage, set our will
And guide us whither we would be.

Mistress of truth in depth and height,
Good counsel's mother, wisdom's throne,
Teach us by light to gaze on light
Till we shall know as we are known.
So prayed our fathers at thy feet,
So hailed thee at the selfsame shrine,
And knew no mother's name so sweet
Nor any home so dear as thine.

We, coming by the way they came,
Confessing that which they confessed,
In their communion bless the name
To every generation blessed.
With theirs and ours thy voice be one,
Thou, under God exalted most,

Adoring always with the Son,
The Father and the Holy Ghost.

Walter Shewring (1906-1990)

Hymns and Prayers for Our Lady's Saturdays:
The Four Weeks of November Leading up to Advent

Devotion to Our Lady as "Star of the Sea" seems to have arisen through a misunderstanding of St Jerome's Vulgate translation of Isaiah 40:15, where his stilla *("drop") for the Hebrew* mâr *led to Mary's Hebrew name,* Mâryâm, *being taken to mean "drop of the sea." Stilla* was then misread as stella, *and Mary became "Star of the Sea" and patron saint of sailors. The first hymn here is especially suitable for young people; the Latin of the best known, the ninth-century* Ave maris stella, *can be found in the Pentecost section (pages 116-7); three popular translations of it appear below.*

AVE MARIA BY "SISTER M."

Ave Maria   *Irreg.*   *A. Gregory Murray, O.S.B.*

AVE Maria! O Maiden, O Mother,
Fondly thy children are calling on thee,
Thine are the graces unclaimed by another,
Sinless and beautiful Star of the Sea!
Mater amabilis, ora pro nobis!
Pray for thy children who call upon thee;
Ave sanctissima! Ave purissima!
Sinless and beautiful Star of the Sea.

Ave Maria! The night shades are falling,
Softly our voices arise unto thee,
Earth's lonely exiles for succour are calling,
Sinless and beautiful Star of the Sea!
Mater amabilis, ora pro nobis...

Ave Maria! Thy children are kneeling,
Words of endearment are murmured to thee;

189

Softly thy spirit upon us is stealing,
Sinless and beautiful Star of the Sea!

Mater amabilis, ora pro nobis…

AVE MARIS STELLA

Ave Maris Stella 66.66. *C. Ett, Cantica Sacra, 1840*

STAR of ocean, lead us;
God for Mother claims thee,
Ever-Virgin names thee;
Gate of heaven, speed us.

AVE to thee crying
Gabriel went before us;
Peace do thou restore us,
EVA's knot untying.

Loose the bonds that chain us,
Darkened eyes enlighten,
Clouded prospects brighten,
Heavenly mercies gain us.

For thy sons thou carest;
Offer Christ our praying—

190

Still thy word obeying—
Whom on earth thou barest.
Purer, kinder maiden
God did never fashion;
Pureness and compassion
Grant to hearts sin-laden.

From that sin release us,
Shield us, heavenward faring;—
Heaven, that is but sharing
In thy joy with Jesus.

Honour, praise and merit
To our God address we;
Three in One confess we,
Father, Son, and Spirit.

Trans. R. A. Knox

PRAYER OF ST JOHN OF THE CROSS

MOST holy Mary, Virgin of virgins, shrine of the most Holy Trinity, Joy of the angels, sure Refuge of sinners, take pity on our sorrows, mercifully accept our sighs, and appease the wrath of thy most holy Son.

PRAYER IN HONOUR OF OUR LADY, REFUGE OF SINNERS

ALMIGHTY and merciful God, who didst appoint the blessed, ever-virgin Mary to be the refuge and help of sinners, grant that under her protection we may be delivered from all guilt, and obtain the happiness which thy mercy brings: through Christ our Lord. Amen.

Laudes   65.65.D.   *J. Richardson (1816-79)*

HAIL, thou star of ocean,
Portal of the sky;
Ever Virgin Mother
Of the Lord most high.
Oh! by Gabriel's AVE,
Uttered long ago,
EVA's name reversing,
'Stablish peace below.

Break the captive's fetters:
Light on blindness pour;
All our ills expelling,
Every bliss implore.
Show thyself a Mother;

192

Offer him our sighs,
Who for us incarnate
Did not thee despise.
Virgin of all virgins,
To thy shelter take us;
Gentlest of the gentle,
Chaste and gentle make us.
Still, as on we journey
Help our weak endeavour;
Till with thee and Jesus
We rejoice for ever.

Through the highest heaven,
To the almighty Three,
Father, Son, and Spirit,
One same glory be.
Trans. E. Caswall (1814-78)

STAR of sea and ocean,
Gateway to man's haven,
Mother of our Maker,
Hear our pray'r, O Maiden.

Welcoming the Ave
Of God's simple greeting,
You have borne a Saviour
Far beyond all dreaming.

Loose the bonds that hold us
Bound in sin's own blindness,
That with eyes now open'd
God's own light may guide us.

Show yourself our mother;
He will hear your pleading,
Whom your womb has sheltered
And whose hand brings healing.
Gentlest of all virgins,
That our love be faithful,
Keep us from all evil,
gentle, strong and grateful.

Guard us through life's dangers,
never turn and leave us,
may our hope find harbour
in the calm of Jesus.

Sing to God our Father
Through the Son who saves us,
Joyful in the Spirit,
Everlasting praises.

Trans. Ralph Wright, O.S.B. (b. 1946)

PRAYER TO OUR LADY OF CONSOLATION

O GOD, through the Virgin Mary
you sent your people the true consolation, Jesus Christ.
Grant that we, who venerate her
under the title of Our Lady of Consolation,
may be associated with her in the work of redemption.
Through Christ our Lord. Amen.

℣. Grace is poured forth on thy lips.
℟. Therefore hath the Lord blessed thee for ever.

(An icon of Our Lady known as La Consolata has been venerated in Turin

at least since the eleventh century, and a church was built there especially to hold it in 1682. The Archconfraternity of Our Lady of Consolation, under the spiritual direction of the Augustinian Friars, has its seat at the church of St Augustine in Rome. The devotion has its origin in a supposed apparition of the Virgin to St Monica, Augustine's mother.)

OTHER HYMNS

O GLORIOSA virginum,
sublimis inter sidera;
Qui te creavit, parvulum
Lactente nutris ubere.

O Queen of all the virgin choir!
Enthron'd above the starry sky!
Who with thy bosom's milk didst feed
Thy own Creator, Lord most high.

Quod Heva tristis abstulit,
Tu reddis almo germine;
Intrent ut astra flebiles,
Coeli recludis cardines.

What man had lost in hapless Eve,
Thy sacred womb to man restores,
Thou to the wretched here beneath
Hast open'd heaven's eternal doors.

Tu regis alti janua,
Et aula lucis fulgida:
Vitam datam per Virginem,
Gentes redemptae, plaudite.

Hail, O refulgent Hall of light!
Hail, Gate august of heaven's high King!

Through thee redeem'd to endless life,
Thy praise let all the nations sing.

Jesu, tibi sit gloria,
Qui natus es de Virgine,
Cum Patre et almo Spiritu,
In sempiterna saecula. Amen

O Jesu! born of Virgin bright,
Immortal glory be to thee;
Praise to the Father infinite
And Holy Ghost eternally. Amen.
To be said or sung at Lauds

MEMENTO, rerum Conditor,
Nostri quod olim corporis,
Sacrata ab alvo Virginis
Nascendo, formam sumpseris.

Remember, O Creator Lord!
That in the Virgin's sacred womb
Thou wast conceived, and of her flesh
Didst our mortality assume.

Maria, Mater gratiae,
Dulcis Parens clementiae,
Tu nos ab hoste protege,
Et mortis hora suscipe.

Mother of grace, O Mary blest!
To thee, sweet font of love, we fly;
Shield us through life, and take us hence
To thy dear bosom when we die.

Jesu, tibi sit gloria,
Qui natus es de Virgine,
Cum Patre, et almo Spiritu,
In sempiterna saecula. Amen.
O Jesu! born of Virgin bright!
Immortal glory be to thee;
Praise to the Father infinite,
And Holy Ghost eternally. Amen.

To be said or sung at Prime, Terce, Sext, None, and Compline

O MARIA piisima,
Stella maris clarissima,
Mater misericordiae
Et aula pudicitiae,

O Mary, star that lovingly
In fair light shinest oe'r the sea,
Mother of perfect clemency
And hall of purest chastity,

Ora pro me ad Dominum
Et Jesum tuum Filium,
Ut me a malis eruat,
Bonis gaudere faciat.

Remember me before the Lord,
Jesus thy Son, the Christ of God;
My soul from every evil guard,
And bring me to thy blest reward.

197

A vitio evacuet,
Virtutibus corroboret,
Tranquillitatem tribuat
Et in pace custodiat.

Grant me from every ill release,
Of every virtue grant increase,
Bestow on me thy perfect peace,
And keep my heart in quietness.

Cum venerit vitae finis
Veni te praebe oculis
Ut tunc terrorem Sathanae
Per te queamus evadere.

And when my life is ending here,
Do thou before mine eyes appear,
That with thy counsel I may know
To 'scape the terror of the foe.

Conductricem te habeam
Redeundi ad patriam,
Ne callidus diabolus
Viam perturbet invidus,

O Maid, vouchsafe to lead my feet
Unto the Father's blissful seat,
Lest Satan by some envious wile
My steps from the right way beguile.
Subiiciendo plurima
Et falsa quoque crimina,
Donec reddar praeposito
Michaeli Archangelo,

AUTUMN

That from my many stains abhorred
Of sinning I may be restored
To Michael, of the heavenly guard
The Archangelic prince and Lord,

Cuius constat officio
A maligno diabolo
Dignos quosque eripere
Et pardiso reddere.

Whose might in the celestial tower
Is strong from every evil power
To save the faithful and the blest
And bring them to eternal rest.

An evening prayer to Our Lady.
From a fifteenth-century MS preserved at Mantua

❧

21 November
21 November
The Presentation of Our Lady

This feast derives from the second-century Protevangelium of James, which borrowed the story of the birth of Samuel in 1 Samuel 1:1-28 and applied it to Mary's parents, traditionally named Joachim and Anne. They are accordingly said to have remained childless until past Anne's natural child-bearing age and to have promised to dedicate Mary in the temple as a reward for the late gift of her birth. This is said to have taken place when she was three years old.

The feast emerged in the sixth century in the East and spread to the West. It was being celebrated in England by the eleventh century and in France by the fourteenth. After the 1969 Calendar reform it ranks as a memorial.

ADORNA thalamum tuum, Sion, et suspice Regem Christum: amplectere Mariam, quae est caelestis porta: ipsa enim portat Regem gloriae novi luminis: subsistit Virgo, adducens manibus Filium ante luciferum genitum: quem accipiens Simeon in ulnas suas, praedicavit populis Dominum eum esse vitae et mortis et Salvatorem mundi.

Sion, adorn your bridal bower and welcome Mary with open arms, for she it is who brings us heaven. She comes bringing our new light, the King of Glory. She stands there, a virgin,

200

holding in her hands and offering her Son, born before the day-star was created. And Simeon takes the child in his arms and proclaims to all the people that this is the Lord of life and death, the Saviour of the world.

NOVENA PRAYER

O INCOMPARABLE Virgin, destined from all eternity to become the living temple of the Most High; permit us to remind thee of that entire, fervent, and most perfect oblation thou didst offer of thyself on the day of thy presentation in the temple. Obtain for us a share in the dispositions of thy heart, when, though a child in years, thou wert already far advanced in eminent holiness, and "forgetting thy people and thy father's house," didst enter the temple to live for God, and for him alone; we beseech thee by the singular graces bestowed on thee then, to employ thy powerful intercession in this Novena....

Listen, O ever blessed Virgin, to our petition, and obtain for us also the true spirit of an interior life, that the Heart of Jesus may henceforward be our refuge and our dwelling. Let us commemorate thy consecration of thyself to God on the day of thy presentation, by a fervent renewal of our vows, and following thy example, may we leave all, in heart and will, to find all in Christ; obtain for us grace to love God ardently, and all creatures for his sake; may his adorable will be ours, and may every exertion of mind and body be happily consecrated to the promotion of his greater honour and glory. Amen.

From the Choir Manual of the Little Office of the B.V.M.
Recited in choir after Vespers from 12 to 21 November

PRAYER

DEARLY beloved Mother, how close to God you are, and how utterly filled with him! In the measure that we know

God, we remind ourselves of you. Mother of God, obtain for me the grace of loving my Jesus; obtain for me the grace of loving you!
HYMN

St Ambrose   *L. M. La Feillée, Méthode du Plainchant, 1782*

QUEM terra, pontus, sidera,
Colunt, adorant, praedicant,
Trinam regentem machinam
Claustrum Mariae bajulat.

Cui Luna, Sol, et omnia
Deserviunt per tempora,
Perfusa coeli gratia,
Gestant Puellae viscera.

Beata Mater, munere,
Cujus supernus Artifex,
Mundum pugillo continens,
Ventris sub arca clausus est.

AUTUMN

Beata coeli nuntio,
Fecunda Sancto Spiritu,
Desideratus Gentibus,
Cujus per alvum fusus est.

Jesu, tibi sit gloria,
Qui natus es de Virgine,
Cum Patre, et almo Spiritu,
In sempiterna saecula. Amen.

Ascribed to Venantius Fortunatus (530-609)
To be said or sung at Matins. From the Little Office of the B.V.M.

The God whom earth, and sea, and sky
Adore and laud and magnify,
Who o'er their threefold fabric reigns,
The Virgin's spotless womb contains.

The God whose will by moon and sun
And all things in due course is done,
Is borne upon a Maiden's breast
By fullest heavenly grace possest.

How blest that Mother, in whose shrine
The great Artificer divine,
Whose hand contains the earth and sky,
Vouchsafed, as in his ark, to lie!

Blest, in the message Gabriel brought;
Blest, by the work the Spirit wrought:
From whom the great Desire of earth
Took human flesh and human birth.

All honour, laud, and glory be,
O Jesu, Virgin-born, to thee!
All glory, as is ever meet,
To Father and to Paraclete.

Trans. J. M. Neale (1818-66)

CONCLUDING HYMN: INVIOLATA

INVIOLATA, integra et casta es, Maria,
Quae es effecta fulgida coeli porta.
O Mater alma Christi carissima,
Suscipe pia laudum praeconia.
Nostra ut pura pectora sint et corpora,
Te nunc flagitant devota corda et ora.

Tua per precata dulcisona
Nobis concedas veniam per saecula.
O benigna! O Regina! O Maria!
Quae sola inviolata permansisti.

O Mary, spotless, pure, inviolate,
Heav'n's clear, effulgent gate,
Fair Mother of our Lord and Saviour-King,
Accept the songs we sing.
Thee our devoted hearts and tongues implore
That now and evermore
Thou keep our minds and bodies, Mother mild,
Blameless and undefil'd.

By the sure prevalence of thy sweet prayer,
Incline thy Son to spare
Our guilty souls, Queen of benignest grace!
The sole unblemish'd one of all our race!

Prayer to the Blessed Virgin

Salve Regina, mater misericordiae:
vita, dulcedo, et spes nostra, salve.
Ad te clamamus, exules filii Hevae.
Ad te suspiramus, gementes et flentes,
in hac lacrymarum valle.
Eia ergo, advocata nostra,
illos tuos misericordes oculos
ad nos converte.
Et Jesum, benedictum fructum ventris tui,
nobis post hoc exilium ostende.
O clemens, O pia, O dulcis Virgo Maria.

℣. Ora pro nobis, sancta Dei Genitrix.
℟. Ut digni efficiamur promissionibus Christi.

Oremus:

Omnipotens, sempiterne Deus, qui gloriosae Virginis Matris Mariae corpus et animam, ut dignum Filii tui habitaculum effici mereretur, Spiritu Sancto cooperante, praeparisti; da, ut cujus commemoratione laetemur, ejus pia intercessione ab instantibus malis et a morte perpetua liberemur. Per eundem Christum Dominum nostrum. Amen.

Hail, holy Queen, Mother of mercy;
Hail, our life, our sweetness and our hope!
To thee do we cry, poor banished children of Eve,
to thee do we send up our sighs,

mourning and weeping in this vale of tears.
Turn then, most gracious Advocate,
thine eyes of mercy towards us; and after this, our exile
show unto us the blessed fruit of thy womb, Jesus.
O clement, O loving, O sweet Virgin Mary!
℣. *Pray for us, O holy Mother of God,*
℞. *That we may be made worthy of the promises of Christ.*

Let us pray:
Almighty, eternal God, who with the help of the Holy Spirit
have prepared the body and soul of the glorious Virgin Mary
to be the worthy home of your Son, grant that we who rejoice
in her memory may, by her holy prayers, be freed from all pre-
sent evils and from everlasting death. Through the same
Christ our Lord. Amen.

Trans. Denis Hayes

FINIS ❦ END

INDEX OF FIRST LINES OF HYMNS, POEMS, ANTHEMS, ETC.
(Translations of which the original is also given are in Italics)

INDEX

INDEX OF SOURCES

ACKNOWLEDGMENTS

The compiler and publishers would like to express their gratitude to the following:

John Cumming *for permission to use his translation of Hildegard of Bingen;* Fr David Evans; Fr Denis Hayes, *priest of the diocese of Arundel and Brighton, for numerous translations from the Latin and for continued help and advice;* Mgr J. O. Hull, *Vicar General of the diocese of Arundel and Brighton, for help and advice;* Prof. Kathleen Jones *for permission to use her translation of a poem by St John of the Cross;* Novalis of Canada *for permission to use the translation of the Russian* Hail Mary *by Christine Grainger;* Novello Music Publishers *for permission to use a hymn by Lionel Mundy;* The Sacred Heart Messenger, *Dublin, for permission to use extracts from* The Little Office of the Immaculate Conception of the Blessed Virgin *(1977);* Nick Sandon; Mgr Anthony Stark, *Master of the Guild of Our Lady of Ransom;* Jeremy White; Dom Ralph Wright, O.S.B., *for permission to use his translation of* Ave, maris stella.

The following works have, among others, provided ideas and inspiration: Anon. The Choir Manual of the Office of the Immaculate Conception of the B.V.M. *(Burns & Oates, 1914); Anon.,* The Golden Manual *(Burns & Lambert, 1850); Anon.* Oremus, A Liturgical Prayer Book *(R. Washbourne, 1878);* Bishop Challoner, The Garden of the Soul *(various editions); Editors of Servant Publications,* Mornings with Mary *(A Charis book, Servant Publications, 1997); David Hugh Farmer and Sarah Fawcett Thomas,* Butler's Lives of the Saints, new full edition, May *and* November *respectively (Burns & Oates; The Liturgical Press, 1996); José Feder, S.J., (ed.),* The Layman's Missal and Prayer Book *(Burns & Oates, 1962); H. P. R. Finberg (ed.),* The Manual of Catholic Prayer *(Burns & Oates, 1962); J. B. O'Connell and H. P. R. Finberg (eds.),* The Missal in Latin and English *(Burns & Oates, 1949); Elizabeth Ruth Obbard,* A Year with Mary *(Canterbury Press, 1998); Michael Walsh,* A Dictionary of Devotions *(Burns & Oates; HarperSanFrancisco, 1993). Plainchant notations were provided by Ignatius Press and modern musical notations are from the* Westminster Hymnal. *Bible passages are from the* Revised Standard Version (Catholic edition), *© 1965 by Division of Christian Education of the National Council of the Churches of Christ in the United States of America.*

211